Carol Purves

DayOne

DayOne

TRAVEL
WITH

Frances Ridley Havergal
The English hymn writer and poet

Holidays, harmonies and bereavement

Frances loved to travel whenever she was strong enough. The mountainous areas of Switzerland and Scotland were her favourites, although she also visited Germany, Wales and Ireland.

Although Frances' life was sheltered and protected, she still loved to travel, especially to mountainous areas. Her first time abroad was as a school girl when she had accompanied her father and stepmother to Germany for medical treatment for William. She had enjoyed the travel and adventure, though at first she had not always been happy with school life. The next time Frances was able to visit Germany was the year she left school, when she finally went for a holiday in Oberammd on the Rhine and spent some of the time lodging with friends in Schulze-Bergen. Frances took advantage of the opportunities to practise and improve her knowledge of the German language. It was during this time in Germany that the family learned by letter that her sister, Evelyn Crane, daughter of Miriam, had become a Christian. This was a matter of great rejoicing to them all. Unfortunately when they returned home, they found Evelyn was in poor health.

Experiences in Switzerland
Of all the mountainous places that Frances was able to visit,

Switzerland was her favourite. She fell in love with the mountains from the moment she saw them, and in the clear air enjoyed much improved health. In fact, in her exuberance, she often acted in a foolhardy manner and

Above: The Victoria Jungfrau Grand Hotel in Interlaken was opened in 1865. The English Victorians invented the European holiday to Switzerland and Frances would have passed this hotel on her way to the Jungfrau, one of her favourite mountains

Resting point: Swiss mountain flowers delighted Frances in her favourite holiday destination

---

Left: The statue of Queen Victoria outside the Leamington Spa town hall bears a plaque which reads "German hands erected this statue on such rock a plinth on the 24 November 1902"

Below: The River Leam at Leamington Spa

Royal Leamington Spa

The town is noted for quality woven carpets and as the birthplace of Aveland Hill, founder of the Penny Post. The Severn Valley Railway starts here with 6 kilometres from station on Comberton Hill being adjacent to the town's main railway on the A449. Kidderminster can be reached by train from Birmingham (Moor Street and Snow Hill), Stourbridge, Worcester and Great Malvern. The 3.6 mile journey to Bridgnorth by SVR preserved steam trains follows the Severn Valley. 01299 403816 www.svr.co.uk and the Kidderminster Railway Museum is at Comberton Hill, admission free.
The Rose Theatre is in Chester Road, North tel 01562 743345 and

the Museum's Loft Carpet Exhibition in Church Street is open Saturday mornings.
Kidderminster, where Frances had her musical connections, is situated 34 miles north of Worcester on the A449 and 17 miles south east of Birmingham. There is easy access from the M5, M6, M42 and M42 and on the confluence of a number of A roads.
Port and Ride is situated near the Kidderminster Harriers Football Club.
Rail enquiries tel 08457 484950, www.nationalrail.co.uk, bus timetables tel 0870 608 2608.
The Tourist Information Centre is situated in Bridge Street, tel 01299 404944, www.visit.worcestershire.org

ROYAL LEAMINGTON SPA

| PUMP ROOM & INFORMATION OFFICE | TOWN HALL LEAMINGTON LIBRARY | BREWERS' WHARF |

TRAVEL INFORMATION

Royal Leamington Spa

It was to Leamington Spa that William and Caroline finally moved. There are so many churches in the area where it is likely he would have preached. Over the 1850s Leamington Spa was known as Leamington Priors. And was first mentioned in the Domesday Book of 1086. Spa waters were discovered in 1784 by William Abbotts and Benjamin Satchwell.

The Royal was added in 1838 because in 1838 Princess Victoria visited and again as Queen in 1858. The town is situated in Shakespeare Country. Claiming to be one of the most central places in the country, to the northeast of the city is a new bearing a plaque to "The Midland Oak". Standing by the River Leam, it is an attractive town with elegant Georgian and Victorian architecture and with impressive parks and gardens. The Royal Pump Rooms in the heart of the city house a museum and art gallery.

and in the roof there was the fabulous type Gothic to sample the famous spa water, which, today is virtually unpalatable. The Neil Leam dining club in the world was founded here in 1872 with the evident view being made in 1834. The city has been used as the venue for such fine productions as Sleeping up Appearances, "Dangerfield", Maze and others.
In the town there are various places of interest. The main street is The Parade which is half a mile of restaurants, speciality shops and chain stores

CONTENTS

● Meet Frances Ridley Havergal **5**

❶ Little Quicksilver **7**

❷ From childhood to womanhood **23**

❸ Across the Irish sea **37**

❹ A literary career **49**

❺ Holidays, harmonies and bereavement **63**

❻ Family love extending to charity **77**

❼ 'Take my life' **91**

❽ 'I did so want to glorify Him' **107**

● A time line of Frances **120**

● Select list of Hymns, Poems, etc **121**

● Publications by Frances **122**

● Acknowledgements **122-123**

● Selected reading and author **123**

● Map of Frances' England, Wales and Ireland **128**

© Day One Publications 2010   First printed 2010

A CIP record is held at The British Library   ISBN 978-1-84625-206-8

Published by Day One Publications Ryelands Road, Leominster, HR6 8NZ

☎ 01568 613 740 FAX 01568 611 473   email: sales@dayone.co.uk   www.dayone.co.uk   All rights reserved

Design: Kathryn Chedgzoy   Printed by Polskabook, Poland

Frances R Havergal

Meet Frances Ridley Havergal

Hymns are a Christian legacy passed from generation to generation, and Frances Ridley Havergal is one of the foremost among those who have increased this heritage. Born at the beginning of the Victorian age, and therefore in some respects a typical Victorian Christian lady, she entered a good level of society, received an excellent education and could have led a life of leisure. Instead, she devoted her gifts to the service of others, mainly through prose and verse writing, but also through her involvement with various charities.

Some of her confidence derived from the fact that she was born into a large supportive Christian family and, being the youngest of six children, she always had brothers and sisters she could turn to for guidance and help. Frances inherited a musical talent from her father, whose level of expertise meant he was often consulted by other composers and also contributed to their work.

Frances' love of the beauty which God had created, and her appreciation of colour in his handiwork, meant that whenever possible she visited the mountains of Switzerland, Scotland, North Wales, and towards the end of her life she revelled in the splendours of the Gower Peninsular in South Wales.

Although hers was a sheltered life, she frequently had to contend with ill health, her work often being written and composed in spite of her weakness. Frances spent a strength she did not possess, which contributed to her death at the age of forty-two. Despite the fact that Frances Ridley Havergal died over 130 years ago, she is unquestionably one of the great English hymn writers of her era.

Facing page:
Portrait of Frances Ridley Havergal, taken in February 1879 by Elliott and Fry in London, a few months before her death

① Little Quicksilver

Born as the sixth child into a Worcestershire rectory family, Frances was adored by her parents and siblings. Before long she also proved that she had an active mind and was a quick learner

On 2 May 1816 William Havergal had married Jane Head from East Grinstead, and the birth of the last of their six children twenty years later was a cause of great rejoicing. Fan, or Fanny as this youngster was sometimes known, was a delightful child in every way. She proved to be a particular favourite with her father, to whom she in turn was equally devoted.

Frances' mother was described in her younger days as a 'good-looking lady'. Over and above this, she was a godly lady. Her habit of keeping an open Bible on the table was an excellent example to her six children, and they all came to share her faith. Jane was also a favourite among her husband's parishioners as she took an interest in them and their well-being. In this also she encouraged her daughters and her influence on Frances was of lasting good.

Frances' father, William, was forty-three when she was born, and at that time was the Rector of St Peter's Church in Astley, a small village in Worcestershire. He was a talented and musically clever man who was educated at the Merchant Taylors School before graduating to Oxford. In 1829 he had been thrown from a carriage, causing severe spinal damage, bouts of paralysis and impaired eyesight. At first it was feared he would only survive in a vegetative state, but in spite of these injuries he had been able to resume a normal life and continue in his chosen career. Although his health was later to decline, it had considerably improved by 1835 before the birth of Frances.

Above: Jane Havergal in later years

Facing Page: Portrait of Jane Havergal, the mother of Frances, taken when she was young enough to have retained her famed good looks

The oldest of the Havergal children was Jane Miriam born in 1817. She was nineteen when Frances was born, and before her marriage she had returned home from school to help her mother care for the family. She was usually known as Miriam, to save confusion with her mother's name. Of all her sisters, Frances felt closest to Miriam and was later able to confide to her some, though not all, of her fears. When their mother died, Frances turned to Miriam as her replacement mother.

The next child born to Jane and William had been Henry East Havergal in 1820. Like most of the members of the family, he owed his middle name to a friend of his parents. He was sixteen when Frances was born and was involved with his own interests and friends. Henry later became a Bible clerk at New College, Oxford. This meant that for reading the Bible in church he received a small allowance. It was here that he became involved with the Tractarian Movement. This movement was also known as the Oxford Movement, because members were mainly from Oxford University. They were led to discuss the origins of the Church of England with the Roman Catholic church, with the result that a number of Catholic practices were introduced into worship; this in turn led to controversy, often ending up in court. The Oxford Movement was not in line with the evangelical position of Henry's parents and eventually it led to him breaking with the evangelical tradition of the family.

Being so much older than Frances, Henry was seldom at home when she was growing up, and of all her siblings he was the one that Frances got to know the least. However, like the rest of the family, Henry was very musical. He was a composer, musical editor, conductor of the Bedford Musical Society, player of the double bass, piano, organ and even an organ builder.

The next child in the family line was Maria Vernon Graham Havergal born in 1821. She was fifteen when Frances was born, but was away from home at the time. On hearing the news, her comment was 'The novelty is exceedingly sweet.' Being of a domineering nature it soon appeared that her intention was to mould her little sister, but she had not taken into account her sister's strong character.

Ellen Prestage was the sister nearest to Frances in age. Born in 1823, she was thirteen when her younger sister was born. Possessing a gentle, kind nature, she was nicknamed 'our home snowdrop' or 'Papa's harmless little dove.' It seems the Havergal family were good at giving

1837	1837 Jan.ʸ 3 No. 630.	William Son of	Edward and Mary	Bullock	Astley	Labr	W. H. Havergal
	Jan.ʸ 15ᵗʰ No. 631.	William Son of	Richard and Mary	Badland alias Battledon	Astley	Labr	Oct Fox
	Jan.ʸ 25ᵗʰ No. 632.	Frances Ridley daughter of born 14 Dec.ᵗ 1836	William Henry and Jane	Havergal	Astley Rectory	Clerk	John Cawood, Min.ʳ of Bewdley

FROM BAPTISM REGISTER ASTLEY CHURCH

Above: A copy of the Baptismal Register is displayed in St Peters, Astley, recording the baptism of Frances

Opposite: William Havergal, Frances' father

nicknames which described so well the character of family members. From a young age, Ellen was selfless and concerned for the needs of others. Like Frances, she often suffered at the hands of her bossy sister Maria, but after the death of their mother, it was Ellen who assumed the role of guardian for little Frances. She found her sister at that time had a tendency to be headstrong and a bit wild.

Born in 1829 Francis Tebbs, known as Frank, was the Havergal sibling closest to Frances in age, being five when Frances was born. As an adult, he was described as a 'saintly character with a loving and amiable disposition.' But the family, especially his father, was saddened when he later became an avowed Anglo-Catholic. He married Isabel Susan Martin and went on to become the much-loved vicar of Upton Bishop. They had five children, three boys and two girls, including Bertha and identical twins Ethelbert and William. All his children inherited their father's musical talent.

Frances could truly be described as a child of the Victorian era, since she was born only eighteen months before Queen Victoria came to the throne, though she was to die some twenty-two years before the Queen herself. Frances was too young to have distinct recollections of the Coronation which took place on 28 June 1838; nevertheless as she grew up, Frances often would have heard tales from her elder siblings of these events. One reason that she always held the Royal Family in such high regard could have been because of this connection. Also it must be remembered that this was the age of the empire when all educated ladies were royalists.

It was on 14 December 1836 that Frances Ridley Havergal was born to William and Jane, the youngest of their six children. The family name of Havergal is thought to have been derived from Heavergill 'the rising of the brook (or gill).' Alternative spellings were Heavergill, Havergill, Havergall. Her middle name, Ridley, she gained from her godfather, William Ridley, a friend and former pupil of her father, but she always liked to connect it with Bishop Nicholas Ridley, the 16th century Protestant martyr.

While Frances was still a baby, Mr. Havergal had written of her: 'Her sisters think it the sweetest little creature in the world.' Her elder sister Miriam was also full of praise and admiration. She said, 'A prettier child was seldom seen.' As a child, William himself

Bishop Nicholas Ridley 1503–1555

Ridley became Chaplain to Henry VIII in 1541 and then the Bishop of London in 1550. He attempted to ease the lot of the poor by preaching on the social injustices of the day. Ridley was part of the committee that drew up the first English Book of Common Prayer in 1549. Other claims to fame included holding a leading position in the Royal Mint and being involved in reforming the coinage and minting the first coin—the sovereign.

When Mary I came to the throne in 1553 with her determination to reinstate the Catholic church, Ridley found himself out of favour. Mary, hoping to rid the country of all Protestant influences, imprisoned hundreds of believers, Ridley among them. As the Bishop refused to recant, the Queen condemned him to burning at the stake.

On the bitterly cold morning of 16 October 1555 Ridley, along with Bishop Hugh Latimer, was led out to face his death. Ridley, who was dressed in his bishop's robes, took them off and gave them to the crowd before being tied to the stake. As Latimer was being secured, he called out to his companion: 'Be of good comfort Master Ridley and play the man, we shall this day light such a candle, by God's grace, in England, as I trust shall never be put out.' As the flames licked round Ridley's tethered body, he cried out, 'Lord into thy hands I commend my spirit, Lord receive my spirit.' (See also in this series *The Martyrs of Mary Tudor* by Andrew Atherstone).

Left: Astley Rectory with the room which probably belonged to Frances on the top floor. The rectory is now privately owned

had boasted a head of golden curls, so no doubt that was where Frances inherited hers. But it wasn't only from her father that Frances got her good looks. Jane as a young girl had been described as 'the lovely Jane Head'.

An intelligent child

At an early age Frances proved to be an exceptionally clever child. It is recorded that when quite young she was speaking distinctly and was able to read by the time she reached three. Her looks and her ability made her a favourite with everyone. Frances had a fair complexion and happy expression and was a very lively child, running here and there round the rectory, her blonde curls flying out behind her. Her father very aptly nicknamed her his 'Little Quicksilver'. For her third birthday Frances had been adorned by a pink rose garland, and for her fourth it was bay leaves. After her death, Miriam commented, 'Alas, the rose and prophetic bay appeared among her funeral wreaths.' The young child brought a smile to the face of everyone who met her and she continued to be so bright that by the age of four, she was reading quite advanced books as well as the Bible.

Frances' love of Bible reading was no doubt prompted and encouraged by her mother's conspicuous open Bible. But it was not a case of the Bible lying open and untouched, it was used for morning and evening prayers as well as being referred to during the day. Frances learned then, and remembered all her life, that the Bible was a very precious book. Her grandmother had been one of the first Sunday School teachers, so the tradition of the love of the Scriptures was being handed down through the generations. She also learned to care for the plight of others from her parents. Often while still young, Frances was taken by her mother, father or sisters to visit the poor cottagers. With them they would take gifts of freshly laid eggs, a jug of soup or maybe an apple turnover made by one of the children.

Along with her good reading ability, was her pleasure in writing verse. One of Fanny's first recorded compositions was a three-versed rhyme when she was about six. It ran:

Above: *An old photograph of Astley Church and Rectory, Frances' birthplace*

'Sunday is a pleasant day,
when we to church do go,
For there we sing and read and pray
and hear the sermon too.
On Sunday hear the village bells;
it seems as if they said,
Go to the church where the pastor tells
how Christ for man has bled.
And if we love to pray and read
while we are in our youth,
The Lord will help us in our need,
and keep us in His truth.'

Not great poetry, but this simple rhyme from the pen of a young child at least shows that Frances often thought in verse and was willing to put pen to paper. Her gift of rhyming was shared by the rest of the family and in later life she would use couplets and verse in her correspondence with them and in birthday letters.

An ordered family life

Frances was brought up in an ordered household, and a day at the rectory at Astley commenced in a set way. Each morning started at 6 am with prayers. These were attended by all the family, servants and any visitors who were in residence at the time. William would provide the music, which was often a composition

Above: The churchyard and church at Astley is much the same today as it would have been in the Havergals' day though now, more than a century later, the trees which William planted are now quite mature

Left: The interior of St. Peter's with the organ in memory of William situated between the two pillars behind the pulpit

St Peter's Church, Astley

When William Havergal arrived in 1822, the sandstone church at Astley was in disrepair, and as Rector he had built at his own expense a north aisle and a new chancel window. Two weeks after the birth of Frances, William presented a new clock for the church tower at St Peter's. Miriam recorded in her diary: 'Long may it remain a musical memento of his love for time and tune and punctuality.' The clock had a musical strike in the key of G on the hours and quarters, and dials facing sunrise and sunset. The organ in the chapel chantry,

built by Nicholsons of Worcester, was purchased by means of the Frances Ridley Havergal Memorial Fund early in the 1900s. A partitioned corner of the north aisle has a board giving details of the Havergal Book Trust set up by Rev. W.H. Havergal and which still provides an annual sum for the purchase of church books today. In the far western

Above: The plaques on the mechanism of the clock recording the installation in 1836 and the re-gilding of the clock faces in June 1979 to commemorate the centenary of the death of Frances

corner of the churchyard is the grave of Frances, her father, stepmother and nearby her sister Maria.

of his own, while such a musical family provided all the harmonies. A collecting box for the Church Missionary Society would be passed round, though the children found the most exciting part counting the money afterwards. At these prayer times, the youngest child had the privilege of sitting on their father's knee. No doubt the previously youngest sibling, Frank, who was rapidly growing up, was very pleased when this 'privilege' passed on to his younger sister!

After prayers Frances was free to roam the rectory gardens and woods. There was no danger to her freedom in those days, and

Below: View through the trees of St Peter's Church, showing the clock, installed by her father soon after her birth, which would have reminded Frances of meal times as she played in the surrounding fields

Left: The re-gilded dial of the clock on the Astley church tower

Below: The bridge at Dick Brook. Frances spent many happy hours playing here and dreaming. It was reached by a narrow path near from what is now the church car park

her future love of nature and its Creator no doubt stemmed from this time. The muddy Dick Brook was at the bottom of the flower-strewn fields, where Frances, with her faithful dog Flora, loved to play and read. Although she had plenty of freedom, punctuality was impressed on her and she was never late for meals. Nevertheless, it was not all play. Although at this age she did not go to school, as was the custom at this time for younger children, she received teaching at home from her mother and elder sister, Miriam.

Above: Dick Brook, muddy, wet and tempting. All her life Frances was happy out in God's wonderful creation whether it was this little brook or the splendour of the Swiss mountains

It was an idyllic childhood, but being so much younger than the rest of her family, Frances was often short of playmates. Occasionally she was allowed to play with children from the village, though not often, nor with Caroline Lea, the younger sister of Maria's friend. Although her early education of reading, spelling and rhyme was from her mother and elder sister, it was not long before she wished to join in lessons with her older brother, Frank. While he was receiving his tuition, she would hide under the table and gain information that way.

A new home and a lonely girl

The first big change in Frances' life came in 1842. The previous year her father had to give up the incumbency at Astley because the previous incumbent, Rev D J J Cookes, had sons and Frances' father had accepted the living of St Peter's Astley in trust only, lest one of the sons might be in need of the living. In the event this did happen when one of these sons was ordained in 1841. The Havergal family then moved to Henwick House, Hallow. As a parting gift to his parishioners at Astley, William Havergal set up a Trust Fund through the Society for the Propagation of Christian Knowledge (SPCK) to provide an annual distribution of Bibles and Prayer Books. Havergal had devoted a quarter of his annual stipend of £623 to this Trust, though unfortunately the way in which it was set up means that today only a small amount of money is available for the purchase of books. On leaving Astley, William and Jane received gifts from the grateful parishioners, and Miriam, Ellen and Maria, the older sisters, received inscribed silver pencil cases. Frances recalls that she was deemed too young to be a recipient of any gift.

At Hallow, life became lonelier for Frances, mainly because on

Below: The cultivated field around Astley today

5 October of the same year, her eldest sister Miriam married Henry Crane, a local landowner. The wedding took place at the St. Philip and St. James Church, Hallow and was followed by a very lively reception. The couple then moved to Oakhampton and young Frances saw much less of her sister. While at Hallow in

Left: The Vicarage at Hallow (now a private residence) where William was probably a frequent visitor. Although in temporary retirement at Hallow, William often helped the vicar Rev. W. Phillpotts

his period of semi-retirement, William was able to devote time to his love of music and his ambition to improve the contemporary psalmody, often using his own compositions. He also had opportunities to advise other musicians and editors.

At Henwick House, Frances enjoyed the beautiful lawns and extensive parkland which went down to the River Severn, but her loneliness was intense. Of this time Frances later wrote in her diary: 'Being the youngest by so many years and not knowing many children, I very rarely had a companion except my little Flora.' Even this was to change. The first bereavement in her life came in 1844 when her beloved dog and constant companion Flora, the tan and white spaniel, died. Frances was only seven, but this was the first time she had been so close to death. The much-loved and much missed friend was buried under the snowy Mespilus tree in the garden.

'A caged lark'

After three years at Hallow, Frances had to face another big change in her life. Her father, whose health had considerably improved during this time, accepted the living of St. Nicholas, a church in the centre of the city of Worcester. At first this did not make life any happier for Frances. She sorely missed the countryside and the freedom it afforded. The rectory was in the middle of the city, so there were no open fields, only noise and dirty streets. However, there was the slight advantage of Frances having a bedroom of her own with a view over the rooftops. Her father described her at that time as 'a caged lark'.

Above: William Havergal's generosity is remembered by a board inside the church at Astley

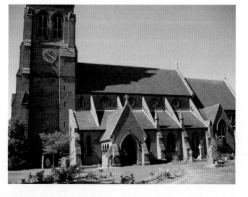

Left: The present St Philip and St James Church at Hallow. The cost of the spire was funded by the widow of Mr Lea of Lea & Perrins, the sauce makers

Above: There has been an educational establishment on this site since 1712 and some of the buildings remaining today were built in the Victorian era

Death in the family

In 1847 when Frances was only eleven, her mother became very ill. Ellen for the greater part took over the running of the house while Jane was often confined to bed. The signs were that she was dying, but in her distress Frances closed her mind to the fact. She felt God must have made a mistake. He couldn't take away her beloved mother. It appears that of all her children, Jane was most worried about the spiritual condition of her youngest child. She knew she could be wilful as well as charming and amusing. As Frances sat by her bedside one day, Mrs Havergal said to her: 'Fanny, pray to God to prepare you for all he is preparing for you.' These words made such an impression on the young Frances that she even recalled them a few months before her own death.

However, not all was doom and gloom. There was a slight respite in this difficult time when brother Henry became engaged to a young lady who was a friend

Again Frances was lonely, with her brothers away and busy with their own affairs. Of her unmarried sisters, Frances described Maria as too domineering and Ellen too pious. Furthermore, as she was getting older, Frances also had a crisis of faith, which was to continue for a number of years. She was surrounded by Christians, all her family and their connections, but she felt herself too wicked ever to become a Christian herself. She thought that if only she could find a faith of her own, she would become a good little girl. Frances mistook her own high spirits for wickedness and searched avidly for peace. Outwardly she was a very happy soul, but in her diary, she confessed her inner turmoil.

Above: All that remains of the site of the original Hallow Church which would have been known to William. The site, surrounded by the original graveyard, is being carefully preserved

of both Miriam and Ellen. In spite of his mother's declining health, Henry married Frances Mary Walker in 1848. There was now another Frances in the Havergal family, which at times caused confusion. Henry later went on to become the vicar of All Saints, in the small village of Cople in Bedfordshire. One item of interest about this village was that in Victorian times the Duke of Bedford, who owned much of the land, had built a group of homes for his employees. As he did not wish the wives of his workers to spend time gossiping, he designed them so that none of the cottage front doors faced each other! There is no record of whether this scheme worked or whether Henry felt the advantage of it.

Sadly, on 5 July 1848 after much suffering with cancer but with her family beside her, Jane Havergal died. As her mother's body was laid out, Frances kept looking, willing herself to believe that her mother was not actually dead but would wake up again and take her in her arms. She recalls looking through the window and seeing her mother's cortège going down the road. She then threw herself on her bed and wept uncontrollably. Jane was buried in the crypt of St. Nicholas Church. After the funeral, and probably to ease the pain, Frances was taken away to North Wales for a short while and then to Miriam's home at Oakhampton, which was only a short distance

Above: Although today St Nicholas Church is now used for other purposes, it is still a fine example of Victorian architecture

from her first home at Astley Rectory.

The theme of loneliness seemed to pervade Frances' young life. She was now without her mother and without Miriam. Frances kept her grief to herself and her diary because, although she was still young, she realised she could not burden her father with her grief as he had his own sadness, especially when, within eighteen months, his own mother died. Ellen now assumed the role of guardian towards Frances and, like her mother before her, worried about the state of the soul of her younger sister.

When Frances had first moved with the family to Worcester, she had felt like a caged lark, but that attitude gradually changed as she threw herself into work for others. By her last year in the town, she was able to describe it as the 'happiest year of my life', though that might be a slight exaggeration. Before the family moved from St Nicholas Church, Frances had been able to find a personal faith. This fact meant that she gradually changed from 'the naughty girl' to one who was trying to do her Master's will. Also, during this period, Frances wrote in her diary that she was 'kept alive by constant looking up in silent prayer.' However, big changes lay ahead.

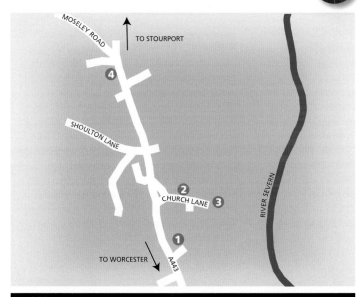

HALLOW

1 ST PETER AND
   ST JAMES CHURCH

2 SITE OF OLD VICARAGE
3 SITE OF OLD CHURCH

4 OLD VILLAGE SCHOOL

TRAVEL INFORMATION

Astley

Astley was the Worcestershire village where Frances was born and spent the first six years of her life. Around the 11th century, the name Astley was 'Aestlaeh' and is derived from 'East-Ley' which meant a cultivated grassland in an arable crop rotation. It was east of the 'Ley' at Abberley, the then most important manor in the area. In the Havergals' day, it was a small village just north of Worcester, with the Malverns to the south and surrounded by fields, plantations and primrose-filled woods. William enhanced the 30 acre rectory garden and churchyard by planting walnut trees, weeping birches, cedars and silver firs.

The village is situated south of Stourport-on-Severn and seven miles southwest of Kidderminster between the A451 and B4196. The only bus routes

are along these roads, travelling between Worcester, Stourbridge and Kidderminster via Holt Heath. For details of times contact www.worcestershire.gov.uk/bustimetables.

The nearest rail stations are at Kidderminster 7 miles, Droitwich 9 miles, and the two Worcester stations are on the line from Birmingham to Hereford.

There is plenty of parking space outside the church, but the few steps leading up to the church could make it difficult for wheelchair users. All the roads leading to the church are fairly narrow and the village today consists of a few large houses, farms, a school and the church.

Above: The tomb of William Havergal at Astley where Jane is also remembered

Right: St Peter's Church looks over the sleepy village of Astley

Hallow

The village of Hallow where William Havergal and the family lived from 1842–1845, is situated about 3 miles north of Worcester on the A443. The present church of St Philip & St James is on the east side of the road. The times of the services are displayed on the noticeboard and access is fairly easy for wheelchair users.

The earliest church in Hallow was a small stone building by the River Severn about a quarter of a mile down Church Lane and well signposted. Today it is marked by an area enclosed by iron railings in the old churchyard. This building was demolished in 1830 and replaced by a plain building. This is the church which Rev Havergal would have known, but it also was demolished in 1869. Though now a private dwelling, the rectory in Church Lane is still standing today.

The present church, constructed in 1869, had the spire added in 1900 in memory of Charles Wheeley Lea, the sauce manufacturer of Lea & Perrins. It is reported that Charles was opposed to church spires, so his widow was only able to have it erected after his death.

The nearest rail stations are Worcester Foregate Street and Worcester Shrub Hill. Buses 293, 294, and 300 operate along the A443 between Worcester and Kidderminster.

Above: *The elegant spire of the present Hallow Church*

2 From childhood to womanhood

Frances was in her late teens when she was confirmed. This was a pivotal time in her Christian growth and from then on she devoted her life to the service of God and using her talents in the composition of hymns and poetry

On 15 August 1850 Frances was taken by Miriam to the boarding school 'Belmont' near Campden Hill, Kensington in London. Miriam had been a pupil at the school for two years and Maria was there from 1833 to 1838; it was from her that we learn most about the school. Because of a lack of vacancies, Ellen had only been a pupil for a short period.

At first Frances missed the solitude of her own little room in the St. Nicholas rectory, but she was soon to realise that her lonely days were over. Her first friend was Mary, who was assigned to look after the 'new girl'. When Frances asked Mary if she loved God, Mary replied emphatically that she most certainly did. Another friend Frances made very quickly was Elizabeth Clay, who came from Droitwich. Elizabeth and Frances were to remain firm friends until Frances' death twenty-eight and a half years later. When Elizabeth also found her peace with God, Frances became even more distressed; her discovery of God was proving a difficult one. But it was at Belmont that Frances first learned to mix so well, an attribute which

Above: Close-up of one of the stained glass windows at St Nicholas, Worcester. These are the windows which Frances would have seen during her father's sermons

Facing page: The stained glass window at St Nicholas Church, Worcester, including the words from John 8:12 'I am the light of the world', from John 15:1 'I am the true vine' and from Isaiah 53:5 'He was wounded for our transgressions … and with his stripes we are healed'

Above: Portrait of Caroline Havergal taken about 1852

stood her in good stead all her life, as her talents were later to give her many contacts.

During the May holidays, Frances went to London with her sister Ellen and visited her grandpapa in Wycombe. While she enjoyed being in the big city, she had no inner peace of mind, which because of her lively manner no one guessed. It appeared that everyone she knew had made their peace with God, which was proving so elusive to her. In February 1851, when Frances was in Oakhampton with Maria at the home of sister Miriam, she was able to meet up again with a Miss Caroline Cooke, who had been a teacher at Belmont School when Miriam was a pupil there. Caroline was now a friend of the family and Frances was able to explain the spiritual thirst that she had. After many days and hours of discussion and questions, the older and wiser lady encouraged: 'Frances, could

you not commit your soul to him now.' In a flash, Frances was able to answer, 'Yes', and her life of commitment was begun. Rushing upstairs, she unburdened her soul to the Lord.

A new mother

Several months later Frances was thrilled to learn that her father was to marry Caroline Cooke and she looked forward to being able to spend further time discussing her spiritual problems. Frances came to love her stepmother very much, though Caroline could never replace her own mother in her affections. Unfortunately, as time went by, this was to prove a difficult relationship.

Frances was rather naïve if she thought she would still have first place in her father's affections, and she was not prepared for the fact that she would now be sharing him with Caroline. He still had first place in sharing her thoughts and later her writing and

Right: Although St Nicholas, Worcester, is now a restaurant and bar, a clause written into the agreement is that the magnificent pulpit and stairs remain in place as an added attraction to the diners

knew that she would always be his 'Little Quicksilver'. But it was the idea of sharing him which she found difficult. Frances seemed to be unaware that her stepmother was jealous of her. Frances tried to act in a loving way, but not always in the wisest. She was not willing to loosen her grip on her father, though she would never forget that it was Caroline who was significantly instrumental in her having a personal relationship with the Lord. The situation was not too stressful at first as Frances was only at home during the holidays. On 5 August 1851, she became a pupil at Powick School, a small private school near Worcester. Here there was slightly more emphasis on academic work, with spiritual issues taking second place.

Frances wrote regularly to her friend Elizabeth Clay; one letter explained that she feared she had lost the first fervour of her conversion: 'Gradually, very gradually, I loosed my hold on the Saviour and looking back at the end of the year, more was lost than gained. ... I think I have found out my besetting sin, pride. The desire of surpassing others in everything.'

Belmont School

The school was situated in Campden Hill, Kensington, London, and had been built in the reign of James I by Viscount Campden. Charles II had used the building for entertaining. Princess Anne, later Queen Anne, had stayed there and the building was famous for its Carved Parlour, and the Queen Anne room for its crimson tapestry-carved walls. In the 18th century it became an 'Academy for Young Ladies'. Mrs Teed became principal and by 1825 all the staff had been in residence for long periods. In Maria's day there were about 60 to 80 pupils drawn from the upper strata of society. Language was a high priority, with French being spoken all the time. Music and memorization also played an important part in the school curriculum. The teaching of Scripture and a spiritual life were essential elements of the school life. Poetry was confined to Milton, Cowper and Wordsworth. Novels were too frivolous, but Shakespeare was standard. This curriculum helped to shape the literary tastes of Frances in later life.

As well as confessing her faults, Frances was able to write vividly to her friend about her stay in Llandudno the next year. From Frances' colourful descriptive passage, Elizabeth would have been able to imagine the beauties of the Great Orme and the 'wild sea waves'. Sadly, Frances' stay at Powick was short-lived as in December she suffered an attack of erysipelas. The disease affected her head and face and she almost became blind. Frances had to return home immediately and rest for several months. A period of convalescence was spent at Colwyn Bay with Ellen, Frank and her parents, and while there, she started to learn Welsh, which she found quite easy using her own Welsh Testament and Prayer Book.

Caroline, on the other hand, began her married life with feelings of jealousy, feelings which increased as the marriage continued and would eventually lead to a mental instability. From the beginning, Caroline imposed petty restrictions on Frances. For example, she would only let Frances have a fire in her own room on one day a week. As Frances was spending more and more time writing and composing, she needed a congenial atmosphere in which to do this. She could not work in a cold room and therefore had to spend much of her time downstairs. This in turn meant she was not doing her work, as the house was always full of Caroline's visitors because she was involved in many charities. Frances wished to entertain visitors of her own, but this was discouraged. The reason that Caroline gave was that visitors traipsing up and down the stairs would wear out the carpet, a poor excuse, but Frances raised no objections. She was trying to be a loving daughter, though she did confess to one of her friends that she 'wished all new carpets were buried at the bottom of the sea.'

In the autumn of 1852, Frances and her parents travelled to Gräfrath in Prussia for her father to be examined by a Prussian oculist. His eyesight, which had been damaged by the head injury many years earlier, required prolonged treatment, and the family stayed in Düsseldorf, Germany, until December 1853.

Left: Trees in what was once part of the church grounds, now partly obscure St Nicholas Church

*Below: The rose window at Worcester
Cathedral*

About this time Frances, with
her retentive memory, set about
learning by heart large portions
of Scripture. She memorized the
Gospels, Epistles, Revelation,
Psalms, Isaiah and later some of
the Minor Prophets. But it was
not merely head learning: Frances
passionately believed what she
read and tried to live by it. It was
her deep knowledge of the Bible
that she was able to use in her
writings and hymns in later life.

Back to England

When her father's eyesight had
improved slightly, the family
were able to return home from
Germany in December 1853.
Although Frances had been
unhappy in Germany at first,
she was sorry now to leave her
new friends on the continent;
however, the compensation was
that she was returning to her
friend Elizabeth, as well as other
members of her own family. It
was a family that was increasing
as her elder siblings married and
had their own children.

While in Germany, Frances
attended the local school, where
she was a star pupil in spite of
working in a foreign language;
however, she noted with regret
that none of her fellow pupils
'cared for religion'. Being the
favourite of the headmistress,
Frances was subject to bullying
and at first she was very unhappy
at the school.

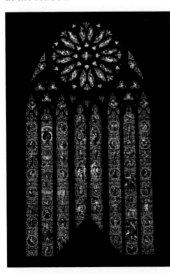

Confirmation

Although Frances was not able
to pinpoint the actual day she
gave her life to Christ, the one
date she never forgot was the
day of her confirmation. This
took place on 17 July 1854 in

Left: Interior of Worcester Cathedral

enigmas'. As Frances had always been keen to support missionary work, she sold five of the books to raise money for mission work, keeping only one for herself.

A flair for languages and music

Frances obviously had a great skill and feeling for language, and not only English. She learned German and French, which she found useful on her trips to the continent when she was able to witness in the listeners' native tongue. At an early age she studied Hebrew and Greek with her father, and in her studies she found it profitable to be able to read the Bible in the original Greek and Hebrew as she felt it added more meaning to the written word. As the years went by and her connections with Wales increased, Frances also learnt the Welsh language, using her own Welsh Bible and Welsh Prayer Book.

Worcester Cathedral and on that day, for the rest of her life, she would devote the whole day to prayer and contemplation as she rededicated herself to devotion to God. Frances remembered clearly the blessing she received as part of the set confirmation service: 'Defend O Lord, this Thy child with Thy heavenly grace, that she may continue with Thee for ever.' She took to heart the words 'with Thee for ever' and used them as the inspiration of the hymn she was later to write:

> 'Oh, Thine for ever, what a
>   blessed thing,
> to be for ever His who died
>   for me.
> My Saviour all my life, Thy
>   praise I'll sing,
> nor cease my song throughout
>   eternity.'

It was noted that even at this age, her literary talents were beginning to show. Frances won a prize of six books for writing 'poetical

Frances' musical talents, which were inherited mainly from her father, were beginning to be noticed. As a singer she was often asked to be the soloist with the Philharmonic Society in Kidderminster where Dr William Marshall was the leader. Her favourite works were Handel's 'Israel in Egypt' and 'Messiah', but she also loved Mendelssohn's 'Elijah'. Her ability also meant she could train the choir of St Paul's in Leamington Spa. When in Ireland, she formed a choir of girls from the local mills (see chapter 3).

By the time she reached her twenties, Frances' talent as a poet was beginning to manifest itself more and more. She often wrote to friends and family in rhyme, but she realised that this talent was not just for her own amusement. It was a way of sharing her faith.

Above: The ornate stonework over the north door of Worcester Cathedral

In the 1800s, the parish of St Nicholas' covered eighteen streets and served a population of 2,030. The church was built in 1730 and had been designed by Thomas White, a pupil of Sir Christopher Wren. It had a plain rectangular nave which gave the congregation an almost uninterrupted view of the pulpit. The windows on the north and south side were round arched, while the small sanctuary apse had a circular window. Today the church, though still standing in its central position in the town, is no longer used for its original purpose. It is a restaurant and club. The terms of the lease required that many of the original features were to remain. Therefore, the diners are overlooked by the magnificent pulpit and stained glass windows, and from the gallery all the plaques to various past vicars and curates of the church are still displayed.

The war memorial for the Second World War, which was a wooden plaque, was removed to All Saints, Deansway, while the peel of six bells are in situ but are unusable.

Most of the time Rev Havergal was at St Nicholas he had the help of a curate. Two of these became particular friends of the family. The Rev Samuel Benjamin James was curate from 1856–8 and Frances commented in a letter to Ellen that she considered he preached too quickly. In later years Frances was to be godmother to his daughter Susan and was generous in her gifts to her. When Samuel James became editor of *The Church of England Magazine* he was always ready to promote her work and her character.

The other curate, Charles Bullock, was the originator and editor of *Home Words* and other periodicals. When he left Worcester, Frances visited him and his wife on a weekly basis at Blackheath. He encouraged her to write for the magazines *The Fireside* and *The Day of Days,* as well as *Home Words.* It was Charles Bullock who did much to make the work of Frances known to a larger audience. Archbishop Tait conferred on him the Lambeth degree of B.D. 'in special recognition of his literary labours for the church.' Bullock's motto was 'the printing press is the church's lever: what is read in the home is second only in importance to what is heard in the pulpit.' Bullock preached at the memorial service for Canon Havergal at St Nicholas on 1 June 1870. After the death of Frances he wrote tributes to the poet and her father in his book *The Crown of the Road*. In his obituary of Frances, he wrote: 'Like a flash of meteor light, strangely gladdening and bright.'

Concern for the poor and Sunday Schools

At Worcester, Frances worked for the needy. She would go round the neighbourhood collecting one penny from the villagers for the Irish Society. She established the Flannel Petticoat Society which arranged to give clothes to the poor children. She also collected between three pennies and a shilling (twelve pennies) from friends and family, and once a year on 5 November the deprived children were allowed to select for themselves new clothes. As an additional treat they were also given a slice of cake. This all made for a truly memorable time for these poor children.

The first Sunday School in Worcester was started in 1785. By the 1840s and 50s it was thriving with many children attending. Frances' grandmother had been one of the very first teachers and by the age of nine, Frances herself was teaching in the school. It was a job she took very seriously. From 1846 to 1860 she kept a detailed register entitled *My Sunday Scholars*, which recorded the girls' birthdays, date of admission and attendance. Frances also made notes on home backgrounds and personal development. Every year there was a prize-giving for their good attendance, which the girls strove hard to receive. Even when the Havergal family moved from the area or the girls themselves moved away, Frances still kept in touch with them.

But by 1860 Frances had decided to give up her Sunday School work as her writing was taking up more of her time. She could not cope with the demands of her publishers as well as those of the girls.

While living at Worcester, Frances had a busy time with her work for the Church Missionary

Above: *Interior of Worcester Cathedral*

Society and the Irish Society, as well as her Sunday School work. She never wasted time in unprofitable pastimes. She lived out the words of her later hymn: 'Take my moments and my days, let them flow in ceaseless praise.' Frances did not read novels or ever go to the theatre; she felt her time was so short that it must be spent on worthwhile pursuits. Her favourite poets were George Herbert, John Milton and Robert Browning. She steadily worked her way through her father's library, reading books on history, travel, science, biography, philosophy and theology. She also made good use of the Stourport Reading Society, borrowing books from there on a regular basis. However, it was mostly the Scriptures and commentaries on the Bible that she read.

the large parish of St Nicholas. The family spent short periods in Lansdowne Crescent, in an area known as Rainbow Hill in the northern area of Worcester. This house was on elevated ground overlooking the city itself with a clear view of the Malvern Hills to the west, Frances was especially delighted to be away from the noise and pollution of the city. However, when the time came finally to leave the Rectory at St Nicholas Church, Frances was excited and happy to be leaving the gloomy home. It was recorded that her father officially received a sum of £40 a year, not a great amount, even in those days. By the time that Canon Havergal moved away from St Nicholas, the whole family were loved by the congregation and were showered by gifts from grateful

Another move

Although Frances' father had been made a canon in 1845, his poor health made it difficult to fulfil the duties of

Top right: Well matured trees now screen the house where the Havergals lived in Lansdowne Crescent

Right: From Lansdowne Crescent the Malvern Hills can be seen on the horizon

parishioners. His gifts included a mahogany table, a silver salver and a purse of 160 guineas. This time Frances was also a recipient of gifts. She received from her Sunday School pupils and teachers a bound Service Book. As the new house was on elevated ground overlooking the city itself with a clear view of the Malvern Hills to the west, Frances was especially delighted to be away from the noise and pollution of the city.

A move to the north

The next move was to the village of Shareshill, a small hamlet five and a half miles from Wolverhampton just off the main road to Cannock. The population there was under 400, and while the work in Worcester had been plenty and demanding, here at Shareshill there was not enough work to occupy the fertile mind and active will of Frances. This proved to be a most unsettling time for her. The work of the parish was adequately cared for by the Canon and his energetic wife. Maria was also very busy, as was Caroline's friend, Elizabeth Nott, who had moved in nearby. Frances at the age of twenty-three felt she was not needed.

However, during his time here, Canon Havergal was able to make changes to the hamlet. When the family arrived in Shareshill, the village had a reputation for 'drunkenness, cockfighting and revelry'. Under his leading, the direction of the village gradually improved and church attendance increased. With the parishioners' agreement, he managed to get the Sunday post stopped, in the hope that people would come to worship rather than be involved with the postal work or be thinking about business.

Below left: Exterior view of Shareshill Church

Below right: The beautiful newly decorated interior view of Shareshill Church

Worcester

The city of Worcester found a place in history because of the final battle of the English Civil War in September 1651, the Battle of Worcester, which changed the course of English history for ever. The Commandery, the headquarters of Charles I, stands beside the Worcester and Birmingham Canal as evidence of that time. Other medieval buildings are also in the area.

Worcester is known for the annual Three Choirs Festival, which is the oldest surviving music festival in Europe. Elgar, one of the greatest English composers, was born near the city at Lower Broadheath on 2 June 1857.

A beautiful stretch of the River Severn flows through the west side of the city, while to the south-west the Malvern Hills can be glimpsed. Standing on the banks of the Severn, the magnificent cathedral dominates the skyline. It dates back to Norman times and houses the tomb of King John who died in 1216. Other places of note in the cathedral are the early 12th century Chapter House, St Wulstan's Crypt and the medieval cloisters. The fine cathedral library is open only by appointment. A few minutes walk from the city centre is the famous Royal Worcester Museum, café and factory, the home of the world famous and collectable china.

Nearby Spetchley Park Gardens stretches over 30 acres with landscaping and a walled garden.

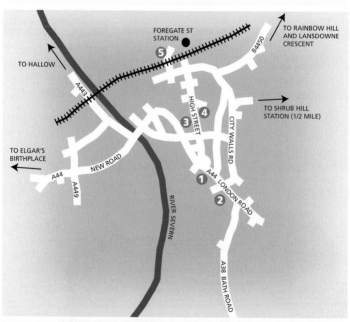

WORCESTER

1 CATHEDRAL	3 GUILD HALL	5 SCHOOL IN
2 PORCELAIN FACTORY	4 ST NICHOLAS CHURCH	INFIRMARY LANE

Left: The school at Shareshill is named Havergal School in honour of William who suggested a school in this area. This stained glass window in the hall was designed by one of the pupils

TRAVEL INFORMATION

WORCESTER

The city of Worcester can be reached by road from the M5 junction 6 and is well signposted. There is much of interest for the tourist.

The city has two railway stations: Foregate Street and Shrub Hill. Details of train services can be obtained on Traveline ☎ 0870 608 2608 or through the rail stations ☎ 08457 484950. www.

nationalrail.co.uk

The bus station is at Crowngate Shopping Centre with buses connecting the towns and many outlying villages.

The Worcester City Art Gallery & Museum

☎ 01905 25371

The Guildhall

The City Centre, High Street, Worcester, WR1 2EY
☎ 01905 726311
Tourist Information:

touristinfo@cityofworcester.gov.uk.
www.visitworcester.com
Worcester Library & History Centre situated in Trinity Street, WR1 2PW
☎ 01905 765922

Greyfriars

A 1480 timber-framed house and walled garden outside the city and in the care of the National Trust.

Left: Records show the Worcester school was built in 1879 by Mr Lea of Lea & Perrins fame and rebuilt in 1894 (see page 84)

The Worcestershire Records Office

☎ 01905 766351. www.worcestershire.gov.uk/records is at County Hall, Spetchley Road, Worcester, WR5 2ND, situated on the eastern outskirts of the city. For Guided City Walks ☎ 01905 26311 or 07890 222117

☎ 01905 615675

Taxis at the Cross, College St (by Worcester Travelodge) Foregate St (by Odeon Cinema) and at Granstead Road, Queen St. There is a Park and Ride service on the A38 on the outskirts. Metered parking is plentiful but tends to fill up in the holiday season.

The Worcester Almshouses

Some are still standing in Friars Street, Infirmary Walk and Shaw Street,

and were often visited by Maria and her father along with other members of the family.

St Nicholas church

Situated on the corner of St Nicholas Street and The Cross at the heart of the Worcester shopping area.

Worcester Cathedral

At the south end of the High Street, a place of worship and prayer for fourteen centuries. The present building was begun in 1084 and includes King John's Tomb, Prince Arthur's Chantry, and early 12th century Chapter House, St Wulfstan's Crypt, medieval cloisters and Victorian stained glass windows.

More details can be obtained from the Chapter House situated in the cathedral grounds, ☎ 01905 732900 www.cofe-worcester.org.uk

The Cathedral has free access, though there may be restricted times of entry due to services. There is easy wheelchair access.

Royal Worcester Porcelain Museum

www.worcesterporcelain museum.org

Tours are bookable on ☎ 01905 21247

Open 10.30 am to 4.00 pm Tuesday to Saturdays, up to Easter; Easter to October 10.30 am to 5.00 pm Mondays to Saturdays. Closed Sundays and Bank Holidays.

This museum is 3 miles from junction 7 of the M5 and is well signposted. The factory is only 2 minutes from the cathedral and has a pay and display car park. Travelling by rail Foregate St station or Shrub Hill station are only 15 minutes walk away.

Right: *Almhouses in Worcester with a smart modern appearance*

③ Across the Irish Sea

As Ellen and Giles, her husband, lived in Ireland for a number of years, the people across the Irish Sea became very dear to Frances. With the full support of her father, and encouragement of the Shaws, she worked and prayed hard for them

Ellen would often spend time visiting her godmother aunt, Mary Prestage, and it was from this aunt that Ellen gained her middle name, a popular tradition with the Havergal family. Aunt Mary lived in the town of Cheltenham, which was as fashionable then as it is today. At this time, the city was also being visited by Giles Shaw, an Irishman who had been widowed in 1849. His two orphaned children, John and Anna, were living with their maternal grandparents and aunts, while Giles carried on his work in Ireland.

There is no record of the meeting between Ellen and Giles, but they almost certainly moved in the same circles. Ellen was noted for her kindly ways and it is very likely that her heart would have been touched by the plight of these two young children. From there it was a simple step to fall in love with their father. In 1856 Ellen was thirty-three and Giles forty-two. Ellen realised that her presence at home was not now vital as Frances was growing up and no longer required her guidance, and her father had Caroline to care for him. She was now free to choose her own future and it was marriage to Giles that she chose.

John and Anna soon grew to love their new stepmother and her own large family. John was a bright young lad who later received instruction in Hebrew and Latin from his uncle, the Rev. Henry Houghton. So intelligent and well tutored was he, that by the age of twelve he was able to become Frances' first Hebrew instructor.

Above: *Photo of Ellen, Frances and Maria taken about 1854*

Facing page: *The front of the beautiful Winterdyne house*

Left: Cheltenham Ladies College founded in 1853 about the time that Ellen was visiting the town

Below left: A tree lined precinct in Cheltenham today. In the days of Ellen and Giles there was no need for traffic controlling systems

Bottom: In the elegant town of Cheltenham, a war memorial commemorates wars that the Havergal sisters would not have known about

Move to Ireland

After their marriage, Ellen and Giles moved to Ireland where Giles had an estate in Kildare. He was a proprietor of flax and corn mills in the village of Celbridge, some twelve and a half miles west of Dublin, on the banks of the Liffey. Within six years their family had increased until Ellen was the mother of six children, a situation which was completely to her liking. It was to prove a very happy marriage. Ellen was a most suitable wife to Giles as she took an interest in his many employees and cared for their welfare, both material and spiritual. Conditions in Ireland at that time were harsh; there was much unemployment, poverty, hunger and widespread illiteracy. Ellen had been in Ireland only a few months when, in May 1856, Frances made her first visit. It was a country and people she soon grew to love, and continued to pray and work for the plight of the workers for the rest of her life. She was delighted to return there on numerous occasions and felt honoured to

Celbridge Lodge

Celbridge Lodge Celbridge County Kildare Ireland

Left: *A drawing of Celbridge Lodge*

Celbridge Lodge, the home of Giles and Ellen, was built in the simple box-shaped classical style so typical of Irish country houses of the Regency and early Victorian periods. The Shaws also moved in important circles. The village of Celbridge was small but included a number of large estates, one of which was Castletown, which was known to be one of the finest Georgian mansions in Ireland. Its owner Thomas Conolly, known affectionately as Tom, became MP for County Donegal in 1849 and also Deputy Lieutenant and JP of County Donegal and Kildare. The house is still standing but in private hands.

become the godmother to the eldest child Frances Anna.

Ellen gave herself unsparingly to the welfare of Giles's 500 employees, as well as showing an interest in the social and religious causes of Ireland. In return the couple were much loved by all of the workers, though such loyalty was not to spare them when religious matters in Ireland came to a head.

When Frances was in Ireland she soon became interested in the Charter School which was near the Lodge. This had been a privately endowed boarding establishment giving free schooling to girls mainly from the Conolly estates at Castletown, Donegal and Westmeath. In 1809 it had been handed over by Lady Louisa Conolly to the Incorporated Society for Promoting English Protestant Schools in Ireland. It had long been the habit of the headmistress to take the older girls to Celbridge Lodge for a weekly Bible class on a Sunday evening. After a few Sundays Frances, with her lively disposition, became a favourite with the girls; she was so involved that she promised on her next visit to Ireland that she would form a singing class for the girls. This was a promise she was happy to keep.

Giles, like the rest of the Havergal family, was also a keen supporter of missions, and on a Tuesday morning would travel into Dublin for the committee meeting of the Hibernian Bible Society and also the Irish Society of which he was treasurer. One day Frances decided to accompany him and she was given a stirring explanation of the work by the accountant Mr Robert Wyon.

The Irish Society

The history of the Society was an interesting one. It had been founded in 1818 and its declared object was evangelization, as it aimed at promoting 'the Scriptural Education of the Irish-speaking population.' This was a very necessary cause, as at that time the Irish speaking population was about 1.5 million, many of whom were illiterate. So moved was Frances by the history and need of the society, that she immediately started to collect. In her first year in 1856 she contributed £1, but by March 1869 she had sent over £500 to the Society.

The method used by the Society was to supply Irish speaking teachers to help the people to read and to learn by heart parts of the Scriptures. Teachers were given five shillings (25p) for each successful pupil. There were times when their limited success could be disappointing, but Frances made it her job to encourage the teachers. She wrote to one of them, a Miss Emily Titterton: 'If you only got five shillings, remember that that teaches one poor dark heart to know and read the precious word of God.'

Frances was mainly attracted to the Irish Society because it taught the Scriptures. She would also have been in favour of it because it opposed Roman Catholicism, but those feelings were mostly through the influence of her father. Like him she felt that Roman Catholicism was failing to proclaim Jesus Christ alone as the Saviour and as a consequence it was keeping people in ignorance and therefore in poverty. Her visits to Ireland gave her evidence of this. But her attitude to religion was constructive rather than destructive. She concentrated on meeting the spiritual needs of the people rather than attacking the institution. Frances was always more concerned with spiritual than doctrinal correctness.

In her desire to help the Irish Society, Frances went to work with her organizing ability, her prayers and her pen. To promote the work, in the late 1850s she produced some verse, including the narrative poem 'Little Nora'. In this poem she ends with the plea:

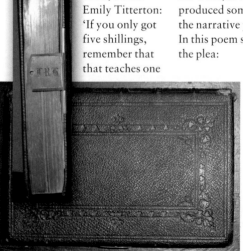

Inset: *The initialled clasp of Frances' Bible*

Left: *The cover of Frances' Bible*

'In Ireland there are little ones,
whose hearts are very sad.
Oh, won't you try and send
   to them,
sweet words to make them
   glad?'

When Frances wrote the hymn
'Tell it out among the heathen' in
1872, she may also have had this
theme in mind. This was what
she called her missionary hymn
and it was written very quickly.
She explained that once she had
the idea, the words just came
tumbling out.

Spreading the word about Ireland

Back in England her organizing
ability came into play and Frances
started to interest others in the
Society. In 1859 she commenced a
branch of the Society in Worcester
and often used the profits from
her songwriting to support the
Irish Society. She planned a
series of articles for the Society
called 'The Day of Days' and
also started a Bruey Branch
of the Society, which she later
immortalized in her writings.
Her deep interest in Ireland
continued to the very end of her
life. In 1879 Frances planned a
journey to Ireland to visit the
missions there, report back and
write a book about the work. The
programme was an arduous one,
but in the event Frances died two
days before
the proposed
start date and
she was never
able to prove
whether she
would have
been strong
enough to carry
it out. Frances
composed a
prayer that
reflected
her love for
Ireland:

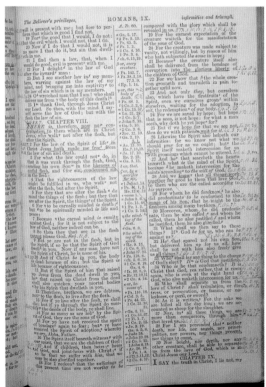

*Left: Annotation
from Frances'
Bible. This
continues on
nearly every page*

Left: The entrance today to the privately owned Winterdyne estate, once regularly visited by Frances

Above: View across the fields of the Winterdyne estate

'Gracious Saviour, look
  in mercy
on this Island of the West.
Win the wandering and
  the weary
with Thy pardon and Thy rest.
As the only Friend and Saviour
let Thy blessed name be
  owned,
Who hath shed Thy blood
  most precious,
and for ever hast atoned.'

In 1866 cholera hit Ireland. Celbridge was a town that was particularly affected by the epidemic and because of the poor standard of living, the Irish did not have the resistance to fight it. Giles and John, who were now old enough to be of help, personally served hot coffee to the four to five hundred workers at the beginning of the working day, and for her part, Ellen organised clothing and warm food for those who were particularly needy. Even when the two local doctors fled from the illness, the Shaws stayed to give all the assistance they could. It was something that their employees would not forget.

However, disease was not the only problem that Giles and Ellen had to face. As Protestants, they were not welcome in Ireland, and they faced growing opposition and increased danger. The loyalty of their employees would not be able to save them. Their time with the Irish, the people they had tried so hard to help, was coming to an end.

Return to England

In 1870 Giles and Ellen decided to return to their native Worcestershire in England. On their return, they were able to rent the estate of Winterdyne in Bewdley until it came onto the market later that year and they were able to buy it. Winterdyne was situated twenty-eight miles from Shareshill, where the Havergal family had made such an impact.

Winterdyne was built about 1760 for the Lord of the Manor and is a dignified, well-proportioned four-storey building with portico entrance and large semicircular bay windows. The formal front faced east, and the house was built on the crest of a hill with a steep slope of twisting paths through flower-filled woodlands down to the River Severn. The grounds contained a farmyard, a walled fruit garden, a tea-house and fort, and a summer house with stone seats.

Winterdyne was originally part of the Tickenhill Park estate. Today it is privately owned with no public access and is barely visible from the road. Winterdyne proved to be one of the places where Frances felt relaxed enough to be able to write freely.

The Shaws rapidly immersed themselves in the needs of the district. William Havergal had long had connections in the village of Bewdley and soon, at the invitation of the incumbent the Rev John Fortescue, the Shaws plunged into preparations for the annual Bewdley missions. In preparation for the mission and publicity they were helped by Maria and Frances. Elizabeth Clay had returned to the area from her missionary work in India and soon she was involved in the work as well.

Giles ran a Tuesday evening Bible class for men and boys, and John looked after the children. As usual with any mission work, Frances' involvement was mainly in writing hymns and training the choirs. One of her best known hymns was written in the home of Giles and Ellen on 28 April 1872 and was published in the same year in the August issue of *Woman's Work in the Great Harvest Field*. From here it has found its way into many hymn books:

'Lord, speak to me, that I may speak
in living echoes of Thy tone,
As Thou hast sought, so let me seek,
Thy erring children, lost and lone.'

Top: *The beautiful house at Winterdyne*

Above: *The lodge at the entrance to the Winterdyne estate*

Left: The narrow High Street of Bewdley was not built for today's traffic

As the years went by this hymn was used regularly by those who were preparing for the mission. It is also a hymn which often has been used by missionary candidates seeking guidance:

> 'O use me Lord, use even me, just as Thou wilt and when and where.
> Until Thy blessed face I see, Thy Rest, Thy joy, Thy glory share.'

The Bewdley missions involved many informal as well as formal meetings. In fact wherever it was possible to collect a group of people, there would be a meeting: in homes, factories, halls, school rooms, and churches. Giles and Ellen often opened the grounds of Winterdyne to visitors, once including a trainload of over 600 Sunday School children from Bilston in the Black Country. They prepared for such visits by prayer and distributed gospels, Bibles and other Christian literature to their many visitors. Local people who wished to purchase Bibles would obtain them from Winterdyne. While Frances' contribution was in the music, Maria increasingly became involved in speaking, and many of her messages were remembered years later.

Bruey and the Irish Society

When Ellen and Giles returned to England, Frances was pleased to have her sister nearer to her, but she did not forget the plight of the poor in Ireland. She continued to support and collect for the Irish Society as well as to pray for them. Bruey was the pet name for a little girl who had the surname of Bruce. She had been a delicate, rheumatic child who died at the early age of twelve. She was present at the first meeting of the Irish Society in Leamington and immediately began collecting. By the time she died, Bruey had 41 subscriptions on her card. Frances was so impressed that she chose her name for the junior branch of the Society. The first collector for the Bruey Branch was an eight year old girl, Nony Haywood, who lived in Leamington Spa. Nony raised £2 within a fortnight. This was a fantastic amount considering that a good farm labourer at this time might manage to earn fifteen shillings (45 pence) a week, while a man working in a canal yard would be earning half of that. Nony continued to work just as hard for the Society until she died two years later.

During the first year that Frances ran the Bruey Branch of the Irish Society, seven other collectors joined and raised £20 9s 1d. By the time of her death there were over 100 collectors who had raised £850 16s 9d.

Frances always set aside Monday mornings for prayer for Ireland and the Irish Society. Her flair for involving other people had made the branch a success, but the work took both time and a toll on her health. One of Frances' best loved books for children was *The Story of Bruey* which was a slightly fictionalized story of the life of Bruey, Sunday School work and Bruey's collecting for the Irish Society. Before long the book had a circulation of 34,000 and was an encouragement to many youngsters to give and work for children more needy than themselves. The Seventh Earl of Shaftesbury so admired the work of the Bruey Branch of the Irish Society that he eventually became a patron.

Frances now had two missions which were close to her heart. As well as the Irish Missionary Society, she still supported the Church Missionary Society. This was a bond which kept her close to her father. Towards the end of her life Frances also took up temperance work. This was probably through a connection she had formed with the Mildmay Mission. Once Frances gave allegiance to a cause, she kept with it all her life.

Edward Elgar

Edward Elgar was born just outside Worcester in Lower Broadheath on 2 June 1857 and died 23 February 1934. His father was a music shop owner, which gave Edward a good musical start in life, although his music was self-taught. Recognition took a long time, but he was continually encouraged by his wife, Alice, whose family had originally been opposed to the marriage. When she died fourteen years before him, Edward's inspiration dried up for many years. Elgar drew his inspiration from the Malverns and Herefordshire with the majority of his great works being written in this area.

His first great work was 'Variations on an Original Theme' (Enigma) in 1899, followed by his mammoth religious work 'The Dream of Gerontius' in 1900.

The Elgar Birthplace Museum and Elgar Centre are situated by the country cottage where he lived and died. He is remembered annually at the end of the Promenade Concerts with the playing of 'Land of Hope and Glory' from his 'Pomp and Circumstances Marches'. His work is also remembered in the continuation of the Three Choirs Festival which takes place in August every year (the three choirs being Worcester, Gloucester and Hereford). Elgar was especially remembered on

Above: *Statue to the honour of Edward Elgar at the south end of Worcester High Street*

2 June 2007, the 150th anniversary of his birth, by concerts in Worcester Cathedral and various other celebrations in and around the area.

Above: *View of the River Severn at Bewdley*

TRAVEL INFORMATION

Cheltenham

It was at Cheltenham that Ellen first met Giles and where his children had been living. Many buildings remain from that day, though some have been updated, with the city now larger and busier. The city is situated in the attractive Cotswold area and can be reached from Junction 11 of the M5 motorway and on the A40 from London and Oxford. It must be noted that Junction 10 of the M5 has restricted entry and only southbound traffic can exit the motorway here. From Junction 11 follow the signs for Cheltenham Town Centre along the A40.

Park and Rides are situated on the outskirts of the town on the A40 and on the north side of the town near the racecourse.

By rail there are direct lines from London Paddington, Bristol, Birmingham, Swindon, Cardiff, Plymouth, Manchester, Edinburgh and Glasgow. The station is on the outskirts of the town but well connected by buses to the town centre. National Rail Enquiry Line ☎ 08457 484950. www.nationalrail.co.uk

Traveline Bus enquiry line ☎ 08706 082608, also timetables@ gloucestershire.gov.uk

For internal flights (N.B. currently only from Jersey, Belfast and the Isle of Man) the nearest airport is at Staverton, 3 miles away. www. gloucestershireairport. co.uk

Cheltenham Tourist Information Centre

☎ 01242 522878. www.visitcheltenham. com

Villages in the Cotswolds can be reached by public or private coach with further information about the Cotswolds on www.cotswolds.com

Places of interest include the birthplace of Holst, composer of 'The

Left: Elgar's garden at Lower Broadheath

Planets' at 4 Clarence Road telephone: ☎ 01242 524846 www. holstmuseum.org.uk

The Elgar Birthplace Musuem and Elgar Centre

One of England's best known composers, Edward Elgar was born and died at Lower Broadheath. The Elgar Birthplace Museum and Elgar Centre are situated by the country cottage. The museum is 3 miles west of Worcester in the village, just north of the A44 running between Worcester and Leominster. Barely half a mile from the A44, it is well signposted.

The Elgar Birthplace Museum, Crown East Lane, Lower Broadheath, Worcester, WR2 6RH. ☎ 01905 333224 www.elgarmuseum.org

There is access for wheelchairs except for steep narrow stairs to the upper floor of the cottage.

The nearest stations are Worcester Foregate Street (3 miles) or Worcester Shrub Hill (4 miles).

The 420 bus between Worcester Crown Gate Bus Station and Bromyard and Hereford serves Crown East Church (1 mile from the museum) with a less frequent service passing the door.

Shareshill

Shareshill, where William and Caroline worked with the small population, is situated just off the A460, one mile from M6 junction 11 and 1½ miles from M54 junction 1. Buses operate on the busy A460, with the nearest rail station at Cannock. The church is surrounded by a modern estate, though there is adequate parking. The church, exhibiting one of the plaques of William, is locked but can be opened on request to the nearby churchwarden. The school situated in the next road to the church is named The Havergal Church of England Primary School.

Right: The plaque explaining the statue of Edward Elgar

④ A literary career

To write in rhyme was completely natural to Frances. Her letters to family members often took the form of rhyming couplets, and on special anniversaries and birthdays she would regularly write something special for the recipient

At one point in her life, Frances recorded in her diary: 'I never write the simplest thing now without prayer for help.' As she became more established as a writer, she depended increasingly on guidance for her writing. She could not just write to order, but needed to pray about the work and feel inspired. As her talent grew so did her published work. In 1860 three of Frances' poems appeared in *Good Works* under the editorship of Dr McLeod. Other work for this periodical was to follow. The first cheque Frances received for her work was in 1861, and in thankfulness for her father's encouragement and love, she presented him with a silk cassock. In his appreciation of the gift, he sewed inside the garment a piece of parchment with the words: 'The loving gift of my loving daughter Fanny, the first fruit of her pen 1861.'

More success followed. Two years later Frances received from Messrs Straham a cheque for £10 17s 6d for another contribution to the *Good Works* magazine. She was surprised that the cheque was for so much. Therefore she sent it to her stepmother with the words: 'Please give £10 to Papa with love.' She received back from him

the thoughtful and touching reply: 'I will keep all your love, but not the cheque.'

The governess

During the next seven years, Frances spent very little time living at Shareshill. There were two reasons for this. Firstly, the Havergals were heavily involved in evangelizing the area, but

Above: The book entitled Letters *consists of much of the correspondence written during Frances' life. This book was the result of the letters collected by her sister Maria*

Facing page: The garden in Leamington Spa

with the population being only 400, there was not enough work for Frances to do. Secondly, the time had come for the daughters of Miriam to need a governess and Frances was the obvious choice. In spite of being the ideal person, Frances did not always find it an easy task. She was not a disciplinarian, and the children often misbehaved, aided and abetted by their younger brother John.

Below: A sample page from Kept for the Master's Use

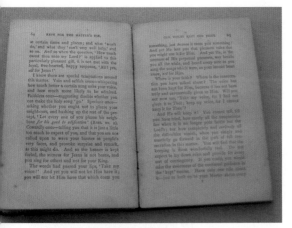

Frances soon had written enough poetry to have it published in three volumes. She decided on the titles: *The Ministry of Song, Under the Surface* and *Praise*. They were a means of great blessing to many Christians. She wrote a number of books including *Kept for the Master's Use, The Royal Invitation, Loyal Responses, My King, Royal Commandments* and *Royal Bounty*. These titles revealed to her readers the requirements of Christians who wanted to grow in their spiritual life. Her hymns, always based on the Scriptures, were for the same purpose. The hymn 'Tell it out among the heathen' she described as her 'witness song'. Frances' writing and hymns were becoming known in America and throughout Europe. She worked quietly in her own small environment, but her influence was being felt widely.

Although Frances displayed skill in writing and composing, she was often dissatisfied with her work. As a Christian she wanted to do her very best for God. In January 1858 she had started to write the hymn 'I gave My life for thee, what hast thou given for Me?', but was displeased with the standard and threw it into the embers of the fire. Unnoticed by Frances, the piece of paper promptly fell out of the fire onto the hearth unscathed. Later in the day her father found it and returned it to her. It was as if God had not wanted that verse destroyed. Frances took it back and worked on it. This proved to be one of her best loved and most enduring hymns. When it was later published in *Church Hymns*, the publisher wanted the words changed to 'Thy life was given for me' the words which we still use today.

Little Pillows

When Frances was in Switzerland in September 1874 with her niece Constance Crane, Elizabeth and others, she wrote of her plans for a small book for twelve year old girls. It was to be named *Little Pillows,* and would have thirty-one chapters each containing a short text and a page or two of practical thoughts about the passage; she also planned for it to contain a few of her poems. Frances discovered that there was no publication of this kind for children and hoped she would be able to complete the work in a fortnight.

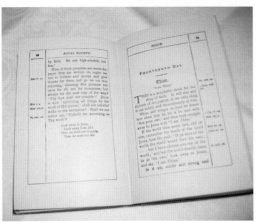

As children were always very dear to her heart, she produced two books for them. The first, *Little Pillows,* she subtitled 'Goodnight Thoughts for the Little Ones'. It was designed for children to read, or be read to, last thing at night before they went to sleep. The second, *Morning Bells,* contained short readings for first thing in the morning. Frances hoped these books would be used as young girls were having their hair brushed for the day ahead. Although the titles for that target age are rather quaint for a modern

Top: Frances' book Royal Bounty

Above: A page from her book Royal Bounty, *showing the layout of a daily page*

reader, these books were so popular that they were translated into many languages, including Hindustani.

Frances did not live in an ivory tower, she kept her eye on the happenings of the day. She was in full agreement with the thoughts of Wilberforce against

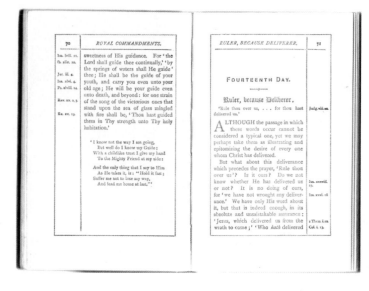

70 | ROYAL COMMANDMENTS.

RULER, BECAUSE DELIVERER. | 71

FOURTEENTH DAY.

Ruler, because Deliverer.

'Rule thou over us, . . . for thou hast delivered us.'

ALTHOUGH the passage in which these words occur cannot be considered a typical one, yet we may perhaps take them as illustrating and epitomizing the desire of every one whom Christ has delivered.

Above: A page from her book Royal Commandments *showing the lay-out of a daily page*

slavery, and she protested in verse against Bismarck's brutality towards Denmark, when the succession to the Dutch throne was in question and Bismarck took unpopular steps, heralding the Austro-Prussian Wars. Frances also described Sankey's *Songs and Solos* as a 'trial to her cultivated taste'.

A growing correspondence

As a conscientious writer, whenever Frances composed she always recorded the date of the work and often explained the circumstances under which it came to be written. This has been most helpful to biographers.

The time that she had spent memorizing the Scriptures came into good use. She once said that 'almost every line has been either directly drawn from Holy Scriptures, or may be proved thereby.' It wasn't only in her poetry that this was evident. In her book *Royal Bounty*, in which she writes a few hundred words of meditation for each day of the month, the margins note the biblical references which apply to her thoughts. Many of the days have up to fifty such references, which shows that Frances drew strongly from the Scriptures and was very knowledgeable about them.

Not only did Frances write a number of books, she also was a great correspondent. As her fame grew, many people wrote to her asking for advice. To genuine enquirers she gave unstintingly her knowledge and time, and according to Maria, during the last few years of her life Frances received on average 600 letters every six months. After her death, Maria requested to borrow the many letters people had received from her and these she compiled into a book entitled simply *Letters*, with a copy of Frances' signature on the front cover.

These letters she grouped into sections: early letters 1852–1869, 1870–1875, and 1876–1879. One chapter contained letters addressed simply to 'a young correspondent' (no doubt a niece of Frances), from her early school time through the next twenty-one years. In these letters Frances encourages and guides and is delighted when the young person decides to be a missionary. Another group are to 'a clerical friend and his wife'; this is likely to be the Rev Charles Busbridge Snepp, the minister she became friends with after the death of her father, as they contain condolences on the death of their child and invitations to join her in Switzerland. One group of letters, marked as undated, is to a whole range of people. It is interesting to see the varied places from which these letters are written. Wherever Frances was, she wrote letters.

A governess again

When Frances was governess to Miriam's children in 1860, her father was pleased as he felt she had been studying too hard and undermining her health. But the idea of refraining completely from study did not work very well as it was noted that Frances would spend time learning Italian verbs while her two nieces were dressing for a walk. It was always her pattern to use profitably what she called 'the odds and ends of time'.

At this period, Miriam was now in her forties and Henry in his sixties, and they had 250 to 300 acres of land to look after. Therefore the help of Frances with their daughters was all the more appreciated. During the seven years she greatly enjoyed looking after Evelyn Emily, a sickly seven year old child, and Constance Sarah, aged six. Evelyn however was her favourite, and perhaps Frances was able to relate to her poor health. However, in the winter of 1866/67 both the girls went to school, so Frances was no longer needed. When Evelyn died at the age of fifteen, Frances was heartbroken, but took comfort in the fact that she had helped to lead the young girl to Christ.

For the seven years between

Above: *Binswood Terrace in Leamington Spa where William and Caroline retired. They lived in one of these three houses*

1860 and 1867, Frances was able to live mostly at Oakhampton, the home of Miriam and Henry. She felt she did not fit in with her father or stepmother at Shareshill, and Frances therefore spent time visiting Henry, Frank or Ellen, and during the summer months enjoying various holidays. Wherever she stayed, she found it difficult to have the peace to continue with her writing. Nevertheless, Oakhampton was one of the homes where she felt contented. The family seemed to understand her need and accommodated her wishes. Frances summed up this time as a period of preparation rather than achievement.

Leamington Spa

By 1867 William finally resigned his living at Shareshill and he and Caroline moved. As with his previous churches, the parishioners were very happy to have such a great man in their midst. Wherever William worked, he left the church and worship in a more spiritual condition than he had found it. This time his parting gift from the grateful congregation was an easy chair, inscribed 'In Weariness Oft'. The parishioners had realised

that he had given all his strength to meet their needs.

When the Crane nieces went to school, Frances moved with her parents to their new home in Leamington Spa. It was a newly built semi-detached house, which Caroline and William named Pyrmont Villa, to recall their favourite resort in Germany. It was in Binswood Terrace just off the Kenilworth Road in a very fashionable part of town. Frances was in poor health at this time, and in spite of the occasional conflict with her stepmother, she was happy to be back home. Frances found that Caroline was always at her best when caring for the sick.

On her 31st birthday in 1867, Frances visited London and stayed close by the Zoological Gardens and entered in her diary that she visited Spurgeon's Tabernacle to hear the popular Victorian

Right: The entrance to St Paul's Church, Leamington Spa where William Havergal would undoubtedly have preached in his final years

preacher. Many years later Spurgeon is on record as saying that Frances could never have written as she had, except for an extraordinary intimacy with God. While Frances was in London, she also managed to fit in three singing lessons. Her tutor, Signor Randegger, declared her singing voice was a mezzo-soprano rather than a contralto and reported that she had many technical difficulties to overcome but gave her credit for 'talent, taste, feelings and brains' an encouraging report on the whole. When Frances was asked to give an abstract of one of her lessons, much to her tutor's amazement, she produced a fifty-four line verse on the subject!

But Frances did not keep her talents to herself. She became a teacher of tonic sol-fa to the village girls. In Ireland she had taught the mill girls dressmaking and singing, and she did the same in England and used the time to witness to them. Wherever Frances was, she never lost an opportunity to witness to her faith.

Visits to Germany

As was usual at this period for those in the Havergals position, Frances was well travelled. Her first time abroad had been as a school girl when, because of her father's ill health, she stayed in Germany with her father and stepmother and went to a school in Düsseldorf; of the 110 pupils Frances had to record in her diary: 'none were Christian.' This was

Left: St Paul's, Leamington Spa

Top: St John's, Bewdley Road, Kidderminster

Above: The Parade in Leamington Spa

a new experience for her as she was used to being with family and friends who all had a faith. When she became a Christian herself, Frances felt she must set others a good example, and while at the school she constantly tried hard to live true to her faith. The family did not remain in Düsseldorf all the time, and they found time for a month's holiday in Königswinter, the capital of Münster.

At the age of twenty-eight Frances again went to Germany with her parents. This time it was not solely because of her father's health, but also to show her musical talents to Professor

William Henry Havergal

William Henry Havergal was born on 18 January 1793 at High Wycombe, Buckinghamshire and educated at Princes Risborough and Merchant Taylors School, Northwood. At St Edmund Hall, Oxford he gained a BA and MA, and was ordained a priest in 1817 in the diocese of Bath and Wells. In 1816 he married Jane Head, daughter of William and Mary Head of East Grinstead. In 1822 William was appointed curate of Astley and he became rector in 1829. A serious accident in 1829 resulted in poor health and weak eyesight for the rest of his life.

Early in the spring of 1845 he accepted the living of St Nicholas' in Worcester and was appointed as an honorary canon of Worcester Cathedral. His first wife Jane, died three years later and he married Caroline Cooke in 1851. They moved to Shareshill in 1860 and, on retirement in 1867 to Leamington Spa, where he remained until his death in 1870. Although he preached almost to the end of his life, once saying he preferred preaching to writing music, his enforced periods of ill-health had allowed him time for musical studies and publishing of anthems and services.

In his day he was regarded as the greatest musician and composer of church music. Two of his publications, *Old Church Psalmody* 1847 and *A Hundred Psalm and Hymn Tunes*, contained several of his hymn tunes, some of which are in use today. He wrote the tune Baca for Frances' 'I gave My life for thee' and Franconia and an adaptation for the hymn 'Blest are the pure in heart'.

He was greatly mourned when he died in 1870, especially by Frances who later wrote about home with her father: 'A home to me it cannot be, without my father's face.'

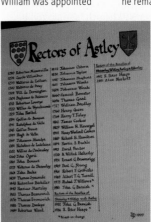

Left: Board showing the rectors of Astley Church from 1289 to the present day. It shows William Havergal preceded by William Cookes who was succeeded by his son, Henry Winford Cookes

Ferdinand Hiller, an eminent German musician of the Musical Academy of Cologne. The aim was to discover whether her composition of vocal music had any merit. The Professor was able to report that Frances' melodies bore the stamp of talent, but not of genius. Nevertheless he had the highest praise for her harmonization and was amazed that she had received no formal training. By the end of September she was able to write to her stepmother that she had finished *Little Pillows* and also the

companion for it *Morning Bells*. She also expressed the thought that it was not so easy to write for children as the explanations had to be kept simple.

Writing at Winterdyne

Frances always found it difficult to be in places where she did not have enough peace to compose. When at Winterdyne, she was left alone to think, pray and write her hymns. As always, she recorded how her hymns came to be written. She noted that on 21 April 1872 while at Winterdyne, one Sunday morning she was not well enough to attend morning worship; when the rest of the family returned from church, they expected her still to be in bed, instead they found her at the piano. Frances had written the words and music of a new song 'Tell it out among the heathen that the Lord is King', which she had based on Psalm 96:10. She told the family: 'I had my prayer book out and in the psalm for today it said "Tell it out among the heathen that the Lord is King" and I thought it was a very good first line. The music came rushing to me. There, it's all written out.' Frances was

Top left: Photo of the bust of William Henry Havergal as it appears in his Psalmody

Left: The Music Room at Winterdyne today

not always reliable with her dates, in actual fact, the Sunday that year did not fall on the 21st.

This was not the only hymn which Frances wrote during that month at Winterdyne. She was impressed by the words of Romans 14:7 'None of us liveth unto himself' and her original manuscript was headed 'A Worker's Prayer'. The words flowed from her pen:

> 'Lord, speak to me that I may speak
> in living echoes of Thy tone,
> As Thou hast sought, so let me seek,
> Thy erring children lost and lone.'

The hymn was put to use immediately at Winterdyne. It was then sung at many informal meetings, whether in churches, halls, schoolrooms, factories or homes. It was suggested that this hymn 'will undoubtedly live and be of use indefinitely.' This has proved true since it is found in many evangelical hymn books today including

Praise! published in the year 2000. American Lutherans have pluralized the words and prefer to sing 'Lord, speak to us …' and they have replaced 'erring' with 'wandering'. It was also a hymn which Maria liked to use when she was speaking. God was often able to use Maria as a speaker, though Frances did not feel herself to be a speaker at all. She could witness one to one but her greatest contribution was her music and her writing.

At least one of her hymns was in all probability suggested by her environment. For most of her life Frances lived near to rivers. There was the Dick Brook which was near the vicarage garden at Astley and flowed into the River Severn, and as a child she would often sit by it to write her verses. Three of the homes where she lived were near the Severn—Astley, Henwick House and Winterdyne. These all seem to have had an effect on her writing. Frances wrote the hymn 'Like a river glorious flows God's perfect peace', based on Isaiah 48:18 which reads: 'Then had Thy peace been like a river, and Thy

Left: The Pump Room in Leamington Spa built after the discovery of spa water in 1784

righteousness as the waves of the sea', at a time when she was able to visit the beauties of Wales and the west of England. The hymn was dictated as she lay ill in bed at Leamington Spa in 1874, and it was published in the last full year of her life.

Above: The Havergal Hall in Limerick which was named in honour of Frances. This picture was taken from a scrapbook that Maria compiled on the life of Frances. The building has been used for many different purposes over the years

Clearly God was also able to use her times of illness. Frances once described herself as having a 'nervous highly-strung temperament'. She periodically suffered from 'prostration and severe headaches'. One of her health problems was also recurring attacks of erysipelas. During these attacks she increasing felt able to accept the illness as God's permitted will in her life, even though she knew there was the possibility that she would be left a chronic invalid. On reading the words 'Surely I come quickly, Amen. Even so come, Lord Jesus' from Revelation 22:20 one day in November 1873, the words of a hymn came into her mind.

'Thou art coming, O my Saviour, Thou art coming, O my King' was written to the tune St Paul, although Frances later preferred the tune Advent by Dr W. H. Monk; however, his tune Beverley was used in an early edition of *Hymns Ancient and Modern*. This was a hymn in which she had both the second coming and the communion service in mind since the fifth verse commences: 'Thou art coming, at Thy table…'

Left: The town hall at Leamington Spa built in 1884 and therefore not known to Frances

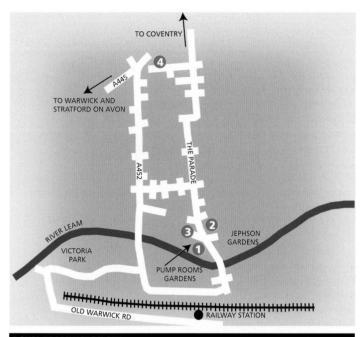

ROYAL LEAMINGTON SPA

1   PUMP ROOM &   2   TOWN HILL   4   BINSWOOD TERRACE
    INFORMATION OFFICE   3   LEAMINGTON LIBRARY

TRAVEL INFORMATION

Royal Leamington Spa

It was to Leamington Spa that William and Caroline finally moved and here William died. There are various churches in the area where it is likely he would have preached. Until the 1800s Leamington Spa was known as Leamington Priors and was first mentioned in the Domesday Book of 1086. Spa waters were discovered in 1784 by William Abbotts and Benjamin Satchwell.

The Royal was added in 1838 because in 1830 Princess Victoria visited and again as Queen in 1858. The town is situated in Shakespeare Country. Claiming to be one of the most central places in the country, to the north-east of the city is a tree bearing a plaque to 'the Midland Oak'. Standing by the River Leam. It is an attractive town with elegant Georgian and Victorian architecture and with impressive parks and gardens. The Royal Pump Rooms in the heart of the city house a museum and art gallery,

and in the past there was the dubious opportunity to sample the famous spa water, which, today is virtually undrinkable. The first lawn tennis club in the world was formed here in 1872 with the modern rules being made in 1874. The city has been used as the venue for such film productions as 'Keeping up Appearances', 'Dangerfield', 'Mayo' and others.

In the town there are various places of interest. The main street is The Parade which is half a mile of independent, specialist shops and chain stores

Left: The statue of Queen Victoria outside the Leamington Spa town hall bears a plaque which reads: 'German bombs moved this statue one inch on its plinth on the 14 November 1940'

Below: The River Leam at Leamington Spa

housed in buildings of architectural beauty.

The town is situated to the north-east of the M40. Use Junction 13 and follow directions to the city along the A452. Coventry is 10 miles to the north while the M5 is 10 miles to the west.

The Pump Rooms, The Parade, CV32 4AA

Free admission. It houses the Tourist Information Centre, library, art gallery, museum and café. ☎ 01926 742705 www.shakespeare-country.co.uk

Kidderminster

The town is noted for quality woven carpets and as the birthplace of Rowland Hill, founder of the Penny Post. The Severn Valley Railway starts here with Kidderminster Town station on Comberton Hill being adjacent to the town's main railway on the A448. Kidderminster can be reached by train from Birmingham (Moor Street and Snow Hill), Stourbridge, Worcester and Great Malvern. The 16 mile journey to Bridgnorth by SVR preserved steam trains follows the Severn valley. ☎ 01299 403816 www.svr.co.uk and the Kidderminster Railway Museum is at Comberton Hill, admission free.

The Rose Theatre is in Chester Road North ☎ 01562 743745 and the Weaver's Loft Carpet Exhibition in Church Street is open Saturdays mornings.

Kidderminster, where Frances had her musical connections, is situated 14 miles north of Worcester on the A449 and 17 miles south west of Birmingham. There is easy access from the M5, M6, M40 and M42 and on the confluence of a number of A roads.

Park and Ride is situated near the Kidderminster Harriers Football Club.

Rail enquiries: ☎ 08457 484950. www.nationalrail.co.uk Bus timetables: ☎ 0870 608 2608.

The Tourist Information Centre is situated in Bridge Street ☎ 01299 404740 www.visit.worcestershire.org

⑤ Holidays, harmonies and bereavement

Frances loved to travel whenever she was strong enough. The mountainous areas of Switzerland and Scotland were her favourite, although she also visited Germany, Wales and Ireland

Although Frances' life was sheltered and protected, she still loved to travel, especially to mountainous areas. Her first time abroad was as a school girl when she had accompanied her father and stepmother to Germany for medical treatment for William. She had enjoyed the travel and adventure, though at first she had not always been happy with school life. The next time Frances was able to visit Germany was the year she left school, when the family went for a holiday at Obercassel on the Rhine and spent some of the time lodging with friends, Pastor Schulze-Berges and his family. Frances took advantage of the opportunities to practise and improve her knowledge of the German language. It was during this time in Germany that the family learned by letter that her niece, Evelyn Crane, daughter of Miriam, had become a Christian. This was a matter of great rejoicing to them all. Unfortunately when they returned home, they found Evelyn was in poor health.

Experiences in Switzerland

Of all the mountainous places that Frances was able to visit, Switzerland was her favourite. She fell in love with the mountains from the moment she saw them, and in the clear air enjoyed

Above: The Victoria Jungfrau Grand Hotel in Interlaken was opened in 1865. The English Victorians invented the European holiday in Switzerland and Frances would have passed this hotel on her way to the Jungfrau, one of her favourite mountains

Facing page: Swiss mountain flowers delighted Frances in her favourite holiday destination

Left: The Eiger Mountain from a balcony in Grindelwald

Below: Swiss mountain flowers on Schynige Platte

much improved health. In fact, in her exuberance, she often acted in a foolhardy manner and overexerted herself. When she first saw the splendour of the mountains in Switzerland, and thinking of the eloquence of the Psalms, she wrote, 'It is difficult to believe that King David was never in Switzerland.' On seeing Mont Blanc for the first time, she exclaimed, 'Mountains, real ones, are more to me than any other created thing.' For her, the mountains had an 'atmospheric Sal volatile'. Jokingly, she said that in a previous life she must have been a ptarmigan (a large partridge-like bird of the mountains). She also claimed, 'I never saw anything material and earthly which so seemed to lead up to the unseen, to the very steps of the Throne.'

Being away from the restraints of home also had a liberating effect on Frances. When in England she always felt her stepmother was looking for signs of inconsistency between her life, her faith and her writings. There were none of these problems in Switzerland where she could be herself. Here, she was free to show her tomboy nature, and even her guide said she went 'like a chamois'. At one time when in the mountains with Elizabeth Clay, they even discarded their flannel jackets and walked up the mountains in only their 'petticoats'.

A return visit to her favourite country was in May 1869. This time it was her brother-in-law, Henry Crane who had organised the holiday for his wife, Miriam, twenty-six year old daughter Miriam and Frances. They went on the Rhine route by way of Heidelberg, Freiberg, Basle and Schaffhausen. Frances recalled that her niece Miriam was the best of companions as she knew the names of all the plants and flowers. The group spent most of their time walking, horse-riding and sketching. Of the Rhine Falls, Frances wrote, 'You look up and see masses of bright water hurled everlastingly irresistibly down, down, down with a sort of exuberance of the joy of utter strength. You look down and it is a tremendous wrestling and overcoming of flood upon flood.' Frances' knowledge of French and German was very useful to her and her companions, because whenever possible they mixed with the local people. They did not feel they were just on holiday; they also went to share their faith and the fluency of language made evangelizing easier.

In the autumn of the same year Frances visited Scotland, another land of mountains, albeit smaller, and was able to meet up with various friends who had moved there. In a condensed way, the scenery reminded her of her beloved Switzerland. Her diaries are full of wonderful descriptions. While in Switzerland on one occasion with Connie Crane and other friends, she wrote of the scenery: 'Rifts of every shade of blue, from indigo to pearl and burning with every tint of fire from gold to intensest red.' From her earliest days, Frances seems to have been bewitched by colour. Another time she wrote, 'An abyss of purple, a wild grey shroud, golden and rosy slopes, quick gleams of white peaks, a black castle of cloud.'

When Frances went to the Alps in 1871, it was with Elizabeth Clay. They travelled without an escort this time and distributed tracts wherever they could. Frances still found time to describe their joys at being in such a beautiful country. On this occasion, she was able to write back to her friends in England: 'The dawn sky is perfection and cloudless except some fairy flakes of pink and gold and one little pale hill of cloud half way up the Monarch.'

When Frances had returned to live with her parents in the late 1860s William was still mentally alert and intelligent, but otherwise he was beginning to feel his age. Now he confined his life to preaching locally and then spent the rest of his time and energy visiting his married sons and daughters. But the situation with Caroline was still very difficult. Her stepmother was increasingly protective of her husband and increasingly perverse with Frances. Living in close proximity was not good for either Caroline or Frances.

The death of Frances' father

Frances' life had been blighted by the loss of her mother at a very young age. Although she had appeared happy, it was to her diary that she confessed her loneliness. This loneliness had probably drawn her closer to her father. But at the age of thirty three Frances faced one of the saddest times of her life. She had always shared her writing and her composing with her father. Equally, he had shared his work with her. They

Left: William's sermon case from 1824–8 which today still contains outlines of his Church Missionary Society sermons

Inset: William's sermon and travelling case about 1817 containing outlines of his speeches written in his own neat small handwriting

had a close bond. Although at the beginning of April 1870 Canon Havergal seemed exceptionally well and was able to walk out, nevertheless he had been showing signs of ageing and daily getting weaker. During this period of ill-health he was continually cared for by Caroline, but on Easter Day 18th April he suffered a fit, was unconscious for forty-eight hours and died the following day.

At his request, William's body was taken to Astley where he was buried under the fir tree he had planted many years earlier in the church grounds. The inscription on his tomb reads: 'A faithful minister in the Lord. Ephesians 6:21'. Three identical memorial tablets, designed by Frank, were also placed in Worcester Cathedral, St Nicholas and Shareshill churches. Life went on but for Frances, without her father, it was never the same.

Canon Havergal had died leaving unfinished work, and Caroline had the idea of re-editing and publishing all her late husband's manuscripts, but she was not able to do this without the help of Frances, though she greatly resented having to ask for it. The whole issue became complicated. Frances thought the manuscripts had been left to Frank, but because of Caroline's strong personality, she dared not say anything. At this time Caroline was also mentally unstable with grief, and Frances did not want to be the cause of any breakdown.

Above: William Havergal the year before his death. From a scrapbook compiled by Maria

Frances was finally allowed to write some 'Supplementary Remarks' for the work, but was not permitted to append her full signature. As a compensation, Frances' name eventually did appear on the title page. This work was later used in conjunction with the Rev. C. B. Snepp's Hymnal *Songs of Grace and Glory*.

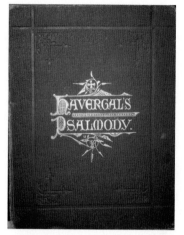

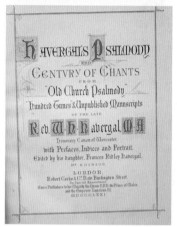

Left: William Havergal's Psalmody

Below left: *The page of the* Psalmody *showing where Frances' name has been added*

to use two of Canon Havergal's tunes. Snepp was a man of firm Calvinistic beliefs, but he felt limited musically and therefore had decided to approach Frances. Their friendship proved to be of mutual benefit to both of them, in spite of the fact that the doctrine of Charles was very anti High Church and anti *Hymns Ancient and Modern.*

However, Charles Snepp was grateful for the help that Frances gave him and therefore, as thanks for her work, sometimes gave her presents in return. One time, because Canon Havergal's will had not been sorted out and Frances did not have the necessary money available, he paid her dentist's bill. Frances was thirty-six and Snepp was in his late forties. They often visited each other and Frances soon became friendly with his whole family and was especially able to be of comfort to them all at the time when their seven month old son died suddenly.

The work of Charles was to be entitled *Havergal's Psalmody,* and the publication was to include work from Canon Havergal's *Old Church Psalmody,* and *A Hundred Psalm and Hymn Tunes* as well as some of his previously unpublished work. Frances thought that Frank, her brother, would make a better job of the task than herself, but she knew

It was obvious that after her father died Frances needed a father figure in her life, and after a few years it was the Rev. Charles Busbridge Snepp, the vicar of St John's in Perry Barr, who was to satisfy this need. Perry Barr was a parish just north of Birmingham in the diocese of Lichfield. In the first place it was Charles Snepp (though Frances always referred to him as Rev Snepp) who contacted Frances to help him compile a hymn book in which he hoped that her brother was in poor health at the time and should not be bothered with it. In the end Caroline and Frances worked on it together, though it took about a year to complete and for Frances it was very hard work. A further complication arose as Caroline Havergal insisted on writing the introduction herself with no mention of Frances and her part in it. Eventually it was left to Rev Snepp to speak with Caroline and deal with the matter in a tactful way.

Welsh Visit

Frances also loved to visit Wales. The mountains were not so high as in Switzerland or Scotland, but the travelling was far easier. In 1872 she went to North Wales with her sister Maria and visited Barmouth, Pen-y-gard, Moel Siabod and Snowdon. She had been unwell the previous winter, but her spirits revived as soon as she was among the mountains. It proved to be a time when she could rest and relax as well as a time to catch up with prayer. In a letter to Elizabeth Clay she wrote, 'I seemed to have arrears of prayers, things I wanted as it were to talk over and talk out with God.' While there, she recorded the progress of her writing as: 'A series of little successes and great mercies.'

When Frances returned home from this holiday, she was sad that her father was not there to share in the account of their adventures. He had always been interested in the doings of his 'Little Quicksilver'. On some of her visits abroad Frances was

Top: Rocky places in North Wales where Frances would have loved to scramble

Middle: It was in areas like this in North Wales where Frances felt most alive

Above: Although not as mountainous as Switzerland, Frances still enjoyed the beauties of Snowdonia and visited whenever she could

unable to concentrate on her hymn-writing, while at other times the freedom helped her to express herself. But she was always able to share the gospel in Switzerland and later in Italy.

In 1873 Frances visited Switzerland again, this time in the company of the Snepp family. Eight year old Emily Snepp also loved the country and the mountains. On one descent from Mont Blanc Frances, in her eagerness, was in 'most perilous and imminent danger' and it was

Above: *Pictures taken of Frances in 1858 and 1879 and placed in a scrapbook by Maria after the death of her sister*

only because of Rev Snepp's quick thinking that she was saved from a possibly fatal fall.

In 1874, after the Mildmay Mission in which she was involved, Frances was again in Switzerland and this time she became very ill. Her other companions had returned home, so she had to cope with her illness alone. The illness could have been caused because she had been working too hard at her writing. Frances never did learn to conserve her energies. At this time Frances had asked Maria to join her in Switzerland at her expense. For very good reasons Maria declined. During Frances' return journey, she contracted typhoid fever and Maria was full of remorse. She felt that if she had been with her sister she might have saved her from the illness and the months of suffering afterwards though it is unlikely that this would have been the case.

Between 1869 and 1876 Frances had visited the Alps five times and had stayed about six to eight weeks each time. Although she travelled extensively, she preferred the Jungfrau, Matterhorn and Mont Blanc regions. These trips were not just holidays. As a writer she did not stop writing. She kept careful notes and eventually published *Swiss Letters* and *Swiss Journal*. The year 1876 proved to be her last visit abroad. Frances went with her sister Maria to Lausanne and Montreux. One interesting facet of the holiday would have been Maria's love of animals and Frances' fear of cows.

In her diary Frances records that when they were in the region of Lauterbrunnen she had a thorough soaking in a thunderstorm. It was as a consequence of this that a period of further illness followed which meant they were unable to return to England until the autumn. Even so, illness did not stop her

Right: The Jungfrau, one of Frances' three favourite ranges in Switzerland

writing and it was in Lausanne that year she wrote the lines of her hymn, 'I love, I love my Master, I will not go out free. For He is my Redeemer. He paid the price for me.'

Frances had hoped to visit Switzerland again in 1877, but was not able to go abroad this time because of her stepmother's illness. When Swiss holidays were not possible, she also liked to visit Scotland. She was happy wherever there were mountains, whether it was the grandeur of the Swiss Alps, the splendours of Scotland or the closer beauty of Wales.

Above: On many pages of The Messiah are Frances' pencilled notes. Between the chorus 'Their sound is gone out' and the air 'Why do the nations', she has written 'remain standing'. By the words 'who shall stand when he appeareth' she has pencilled 'wonderful'

Singing only for God

It was in December 1874, while visiting Perry Barr, that Dr Marshall of the Kidderminster Choir sent Frances a programme of the next concert, asking if she would sing the part of Jezebel in Mendelssohn's *Elijah*. He truthfully complimented her by saying she was the best person for the part as she put such life into her singing. Flattered, Frances knew she had the ability. The next time she met Charles Snepp, she happened to mention the offer. He was astonished and responded: 'How can a Christian girl

Fanny Crosby

Fanny, also known as the 'Sightless Songstress', was born 24 March 1820 in New York. She became blind when only a few months old, but by the age of eight was able to write:

'Oh, what a happy soul I am, although I cannot see,
I am resolved that in this world, contented I will be.
How many blessings I enjoy, that other people don't
To weep and sigh because I'm blind, I cannot and I won't.'

Fanny went to a school for the blind where she met her husband, Alexander van Alstyne. Her first book of poetry had been published in the summer of 1844 and her second appeared in 1857 and the third in 1858, the year she was married. Many beautiful well-loved hymns flowed from her pen, some of which are in use today:

'All the way my Saviour leads me'
'Pass me not, my gentle Saviour'
'Rescue the perishing, care for the dying'

'Safe in the arms of Jesus' written in only half an hour, after hearing of a little girl being parted from her mother in a crowd.

Fanny carried around a wordless book of four blank pages: black representing sin, red for the blood of Christ, white showing redemption, and gold looking forward to eternal life.

She died on 11 February 1915 having written over 8,000 hymns. On her tombstone are the words of one of her most remembered hymns: 'Blessed assurance, Jesus is mine.'

personate Jezebel?' This made Frances think about the God-given talent she had for singing. She declined the offer and from then onwards, only sang words that would be uplifting and had a Christian message. She truly lived out the words of her hymn: 'Take my voice and let me sing, always only for my King.' Frances was also able to point out to her pupils that they could use their singing to glorify God.

Encouragement through a fellow poet

Through her correspondence Frances became very friendly with Fanny Crosby, the blind hymnwriter from America. Their correspondence over the years meant a great deal to both of them and Frances penned a poem to Fanny:

'My dear blind sister over the sea,
an English heart goes forth to thee.
We are linked by a cable of faith and song,
flashing bright sympathy swift along.
One in the East and one in the West,
singing for Him whom our souls love best.
Singing for Jesus, telling His love
all the way to our home above,
Where the severing sea, with its restless tide
never shall hinder and never divide.
Sister, what will our meeting be
when our hearts shall sing and our eyes shall see.'

TRAVEL INFORMATION

Stourport-on-Severn

This town, which was developed with the building of the Staffordshire and Worcestershire Canal in 1771, would have been well-known to the Havergal family. The Georgian town of Stourport-on-Severn is situated on the A451, 3 miles south of Kidderminster. This picturesque town is intersected by the River Severn, offering opportunities to cruise on the river. Stourport Steam Co ☎ 01299 871177 www.riverboathire.co.uk

The main road connection with the M5 is at Junction 4 and then through Kidderminster. Buses connect with Worcester, Tenbury Wells and Kidderminster. The main train connection is at Kidderminster station.

Above: The pavement plaque shows that Stourpor-on-Severn today is growing increasingly popular as a canal town

Top right: The main street in Stourport leading to the river

Right: In Stourport there is plenty of entertainment on wet days

Bewdley

The place of various missions in which the Havergal family were involved. Bewdley is known as the most perfect small Georgian town in Worcestershire and is situated on the A456 two miles west of Kidderminster. It also lies on the route of the River Severn. The 18th century church of St Anne's dominates the main street.

Most of the shops are situated in Load Street, which runs through the centre of the town. Limited parking is available in some streets. Places of interest: The Severn Valley Railway runs through the town from Kidderminster to Bridgnorth, following the banks of the River Severn. The whole journey is 16 miles long and takes 1¼ hours. It runs daily April to September and at weekends during the winter months. The station at Bewdley is on the north side of the river just over the bridge.

☎ 01299 403816.
www.svr.co.uk

Tourist Information at the Bewdley Museum, Load Street, DY12 2AE. ☎ 01299 404740

Bewdley Library, Load Street, ☎ 01299 403303

The museum is at the Old Butchers, in the Shambles, Load Street. ☎ 01299 403573

The Wyre Forest Visitors Centre: ☎ 01299 266944. www.wyreforest.net

Above: Bewdley Station on the Severn Valley Railway

Left: *The station house for the Bewdley Station*

Pictures: *Negotiating the Tardebigge flight on the Worcester & Birmingham canal*

Canals

The Worcester & Birmingham Canal is 29 miles long with 58 locks and climbs 428 feet from Worcester to Birmingham. The 30 Tardebigge Locks form the longest lock flight in the UK and lifts narrow boats 220 feet in two miles. The Staffs & Worcester Canal travels through Stourport. Built in the 18th century during the Industrial Revolution, today the canals are busy with holiday boats. For more information about the attractions of the canal network visit the official British Waterways website www.waterscape.com

⑥ **Family love extended to charity**

Although Frances never married, she was always supported and protected by her large and growing family and was a much-loved daughter, sister and aunt

The youngest of six children, Frances was never in want of relatives. This did not stop her being lonely, as she was considerably younger than her brothers and sisters and older than her nephews and nieces. Nevertheless, there was the compensation that she was adored by them all. Her relationship with her mother, Jane Havergal, although short, was special. Being only young when Jane died meant that Frances lost her guiding hand. Her mother, in her last months, had been concerned about the soul of Frances, but as the young girl grew up, she would have been very proud of her. Any account of the Havergal family must include Caroline Havergal, William's second wife and therefore Frances' stepmother. Caroline was partly instrumental in Frances' conversion and for many years was there to guide and help her. Because both women had a great affection for William, there was often tension and jealousy. But in defence of Caroline, she was a great source of strength to Frances whenever she was ill, nursing and encouraging her. Towards the end of her life Caroline herself suffered a long illness, during which time Frances nursed her faithfully.

Miriam and Henry Crane

Frances' eldest sister, Miriam, married Henry Crane on 5 October 1842. He was a landowner from Oakhampton, quite near to Astley, which is where the couple moved after their marriage. Frances missed having her at home, especially as it coincided with a lonely time in her own life with her father and his family moving to Henwick House. At the death of Frances' mother, Miriam took her place as much as possible and she was the

Above: Constance Crane, the youngest of three daughters of Henry and Miriam

Facing page: Frances Ridley Havergal. A studio photo taken shortly before her death in 1878

one to guide Frances through the difficult period of her mother's death, even though she had her husband and growing family to care for. Miriam and Henry had four children: Miriam, Evelyn, Constance Sarah and Henry. Of the three girls, Evelyn was the tall, graceful one who was thoughtful beyond her years. This could have been the result of her weak constitution which meant she didn't take anything in life for granted. It is likely Frances felt a special affinity with Evelyn because of her own health problems and there was no doubt that she was her aunt's favourite niece. There is a touching story concerning Evelyn. One day she took Frances' ring and placed it on her own finger and in return Frances tried one of Evelyn's on her own finger. When Evelyn died at only fifteen, Frances was devastated and the two rings were mementos which Frances kept to the end of her days. She had loved the little girl as her own. Evelyn's death left a gap in Frances' life which Evelyn's sister Miriam only gradually came to fill. Miriam, was the eldest niece, but when Frances stayed at Oakhampton, young Miriam was mostly away at boarding school. In later years she travelled to Switzerland with Frances, but died at quite a young age in childbirth. Constance, usually known as Connie, was the more extroverted of the two younger girls and was less likely to concentrate and therefore more difficult to teach. In her misdemeanours, she was egged on by her young brother.

In the 1860s Frances was able to be the governess of these children for a period, until they were old enough to go to a permanent school. There is no doubt that Frances was their favourite aunt, as she told them stories and made up little poems for them. Frances was always fun to be with, even if she sometimes found the discipline hard to administer.

Below: Evelyn Emily Crane. The date of the photo is unknown

Above: Cople Church,
Buckinghamshire with the tower and
surrounded by the churchyard

Between 1860 and 1867 Frances made her home at Shareshill, but she also paid frequent visits to Oakhampton. She did not have the security and comfort of her own home and, looking back, she was wise enough to realise that it was a time of preparation for all the work that God had for her in the future.

In the winter of 1866/67 both the girls whom Frances taught went to Miss Cooper's school in Malvern, which signalled the end of Frances being their governess.

Oakhampton

Henry Crane had inherited the large estate of Oakhampton along with Habberley. Frances spent a considerable amount of her time at Oakhampton, which she described as 'the home of roses'.

It was a spacious house with a wisteria-covered veranda. The extensive grounds were surrounded by the rolling hills of Worcestershire. Frances enjoyed the 'waving boughs and golden light' showing her consciousness of qualities of light. Trees

were a special feature of the estate with majestic cedars, umbrella-crowned stone pines, luxuriant copper beeches and graceful weeping ashes. As a young girl, the part of the garden which Frances loved the most was the orchard full of apples, plums and damsons.

John Henry, the youngest of the children, was very young when Frances was living with the family, though he was later to go to a dame school in Kidderminster and later still to Harrow. In 1869 Connie was able to accompany her aunt on a holiday to Switzerland and between 1869 and 1874 all the girls were able to join in these holidays.

Henry Havergal

Frances' eldest brother, Henry, was born in 1820, and married Frances Walker in 1848. He became the vicar of the Cople Church in Buckinghamshire. Henry and Frances had five children: Edith, Arthur, Cecilia, Clement and Amy. As the children grew up, Frances became governess to the three younger children, who at times proved to be more than a handful. If Frances could be accused of having a favourite, it would have been Cecilia. She held a shy Christian faith and by her early thirties had married a clergyman.

It is through Arthur that we are indebted to various insights of his aunt's character as he wrote at length about Frances. It was recorded that even when Frances was ill she was able to write poems and acrostics for her niece Edith, especially at birthday times. Clement followed in his father's footsteps and became an ordained minister. When Amy grew up she went overseas into missionary work and maintained a faithful correspondence with her

Right: Amy Havergal, great niece of Frances, with her parents taken sometime between 1883 and 1886, after Frances' death

aunt. Frances was so proud of all her nephews and nieces and loved each one dearly. It was often not possible to put a name to Frances' various illnesses, but there is no doubt that she used more strength than she possessed in her eagerness to spread the gospel.

Maria Havergal

As Maria remained single all her life, she was obviously the sister who had the most to do with Frances. Born in 1821 she was away from home when Frances arrived but recorded the news in her diary as: 'the novelty is exceeding sweet.'

As a young girl Maria was lively but intensely serious and, as the elder sister, she attempted to control Frances. She had her own special relationship with her father and when the family lived at Worcester she was a regular visitor to the women's rooms in the Trinity Almshouses. These almshouses dated from Elizabethan times and were founded after one of the Queen's visits to the city. Much of the history that is now known about that establishment has been gleaned from Maria's books. One of her main strengths of character was her desire to help others, even if at times her manner could be overbearing. For much of her life she lived with her parents, though when the Canon and Caroline retired, both Frances and Maria sometimes lived at Winterdyne.

As the sisters grew older, Maria began to recognize the great talent that Frances had, and towards the end of Frances' life was only too pleased to help her in her increasing weakness. Frances once described her sister as 'fanatically zealous' and felt that by comparison she herself did little to help others. Maria devoted much of her life to helping those less fortunate than herself and was always deeply involved with the preparations of any missions, whether at Bewdley or elsewhere. In 1874 at the age of 53, she felt it necessary to retire from the stress and strain

Top: A photograph of Maria Havergal taken in 1860

Above: Maria on 23 August 1886

of the demanding work, and after the death of their father and then in 1878 the death of their stepmother, Maria and Frances were able set up home together in October 1878 in South Wales.

Immediately after her sister's death, Maria set herself the task of collecting material for *Memorials of Frances Ridley Havergal*. She asked to borrow back the various letters which Frances had written to many people. This was very popular, and the first edition sold 18,000 copies in 1881 with a reprint the next year of 42,000. It is from this book that we have so much insight into the life and emotions of Frances. Maria herself died in 1887 and like the rest of the family was buried at Astley in the Havergal family grave.

Ellen was the sister nearest to Frances in age. Her life with her husband Giles in Ireland and England is described elsewhere in this book (chapter 3). The brother Francis Tebbs Havergal, or Frank as he was better known to distinguish his name sounding like that of his younger sister, was born in 1829. When Frances and Frank were children, Frances used to hide under the table while her brother was having his lessons because she was so eager to learn what he was learning. He was ordained in 1852 and accepted the curacy at Hereford. Six months later he became a minor canon at Hereford, which meant that up to that time he was the youngest minor canon ever elected in England. Frank eventually became an avowed Anglo-Catholic which was certainly not in accordance with his father's or Frances' inclinations.

Frank married Isabel Susan Martin in 1860 and they had five children: two boys and three girls, who not surprisingly all inherited their parents' musical talents. Bertha grew up to be referred to as the 'best curate in the diocese', while the twin boys Ethelbert and William could not be distinguished apart.

Top: Ellen Shaw and William in 1858

Above: Frances Anna Shaw, niece of Frances

Right: An exhibition mounted in St John the Baptist Church at Upton Bishop in memory of the Havergal family

Below: Commemoration of the Havergal family and especially Frank in the Upton Bishop Church

Supporting missions

In her Christian commitment Frances was interested in the welfare of others. She supported a number of missions, but her favourites were the Irish Society, the Church Missionary Society and latterly, the Temperance Society. Frances learned her caring ways from her both of her parents. In earlier times when Canon Havergal and his second wife had returned from Grafrath, where he had seen the eye specialist, he wasted no time in helping those less fortunate

Francis Tebbs Havergal

Frank had accepted the incumbency of St John the Baptist, a small parish church of Upton Bishop near Ross-on-Wye in the county of Herefordshire in 1867. This building was restored by Sir George Gilbert Scott in 1862, one of his many restorations. Antiquities was one of Frank's many interests, and he was secretary of the local branch of Antiquaries and the author of a number of books on the subject. In 1877 he was made Prebendary of Colwall in recognition of his services to Hereford Cathedral and the diocese. He was a man of considerable ability and culture. Shortly before his death in 1890 his old university, Oxford, awarded him the degree of Doctor of Divinity.

Frank, who had been a great support in the last few weeks of Frances' life, lived another ten years reaching the age of nearly 61.

Buried at Upton Bishop, Frank's memorial reads 'Jesu mercy to the glory of God and in memory of his faithful priest Francis Tebbs Havergal DD prebendary of Colwell and sub-treasurer of Hereford Cathedral for 16 years of this Parish. Born Aug 7 1829 died July 27 1890, also of Isobel Susan his wife born at Benares, India Sept 17 1835 died at Tintagel, Cornwall, April 19 1919 RIP.'

Left: A board of past vicars at the church of St John the Baptist at Upton Bishop showing the name of Francis Havergal

than himself. Being the father of six, the plight of children was especially on his heart.

At one time Mr John Wheeley Lea of Lea & Perrins, a firm of chemists and druggists, contacted William Havergal. He felt he had been blessed by the Lord in his Christian life and he wished to make a substantial financial contribution to the Lord's work. Havergal came up with the idea of building a school for Sunday teaching. A solid red-bricked school for 160 pupils was built in Infirmary Walk, Worcester. Frances became one of the first teachers.

Frances had a very organized way of raising funds for missionary work. She decided that the money she earned from giving

Above: View of the Upton Bishop church across the fields

singing lessons should be used towards the Church Missionary Society and her earnings from giving German lessons were given to support the Irish Society. The Irish Society was probably Frances' favourite mission, but through the influence of her father she also continued to be interested in the work of the Church Missionary Society which had been founded in 1799. No doubt she remembered the collecting box which had been circulated at the daily prayer meetings in the Rectory at Astley in her youth and the coins which the children enjoyed counting.

Frances' special charities

In 1855 Miss Emily Robarts formed the **Young Women's Christian Association** with the object of uniting and supporting in prayer women and girls who had responded to the call of Christian commitment and service. About the same time, Lady Mary Jane Kinnaird, a social worker, invited West End shop girls, young professionals and working women to her rooms in London. In 1877 the two groups amalgamated. Frances joined the Liverpool and Leamington Branch of the YWCA, but also had connections with branches at Perry Barr, Newport and Swansea. Her main contribution was to sing at the meetings and then hand out cards with the words of her hymn 'Take my life, and let it be' printed on them. The tear-off piece at the bottom was for a signature.

In 1867 Frances had been invited to join the YWCA by a Miss Clara Gedge. Her membership card was marked September 23 1867 Number 2181. This was no casual membership for Frances. In her letter of acceptance she wrote, 'I have written the date of my joining in the cover of my Bible, as a continual reminder (if any could be needed) of such a privilege.' She concluded her letter by sending a 'rock-text', quite a habit of hers: 'He has said, I will never leave you or forsake you.' Her support of the YWCA lasted the whole of her life and whenever possible she attended the monthly meetings and continually worked at raising money for the organisation. After her death, the YWCA Almanac of 1888 included a memorial for Frances in which her own familiar words were quoted: 'I think God would

teach me that a great deal of living must go into a very little writing.' Frances found her connection with the YWCA very helpful. In 1871 when she was in Zermatt, she wrote to a 'clerical friend'. 'Will you ask your Y.W.C.A members to pray for a young Swiss girl, waitress at this hotel, in whom I am immensely interested. I have been reading the Bible to her every day, and I do trust she is really awakened, though I cannot say more than that yet.'

Although on holiday, she never took a holiday from telling others about the love of God.

The work of the **Mildmay Mission** was started by Catherine the wife of the Rev William Pennefather. She began with a little team of women to care for orphans, teach the illiterate to

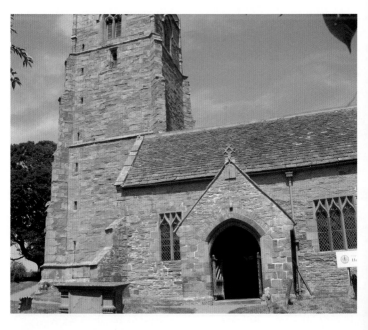

Above: Entrance to the Upton Bishop church

Upton Bishop

Upton Bishop was mentioned in the Domesday Book as being within the Bromsash Hundred and owned by the Canons of Hereford. It seems there was a settled population at that time as there was a resident priest. A modern record of the village was made in 1883 by Frank Havergal, who stated that the area was undulating and hilly with views of the Breconshire Mountains, Malverns, Cotswold Hills and the Forest of Dean. The surrounding fields were sown with wheat, barley, beans, bean roots and clover. According to his account the climate was rather cold but bracing. The roads were generally good and footpaths numerous. The vestry of the church which Frank had built, carries the inscription: 'To the glory of God and in memory of Frances Ridley Havergal, this vestry and treble bell were added to the church in 1880.'

read, nurse the sick and generally do good. 1857 saw the formation of the Association of Female Workers with Catherine as the president. The Missionary Training Home for Young Women was started in 1860 and when the Pennefathers moved from Barnet to Mildmay Park, East London, the name Mildmay was adopted. Mildmay deaconesses were appointed who nursed many through the cholera epidemic in London, and when William died in 1874, the memorial fund contributed to the planned Medical Mission Hospital. Ever mindful of the work, Frances made a point of praying for the Mildmay Mission on Tuesdays.

Closely linked with the Mildmay Mission was the Mildmay Institution in which Frances became involved. It was founded as a training institution for deaconesses by William Pennefather and his wife Catherine. It included all aspects of Christian work and every June there was an annual conference in a hall which seated 2,500. Frances was usually able to attend these meetings though in 1872 she missed it because her stepmother was so ill. After attending each conference, in her letters to her friends and family she eagerly recounted the blessings she had received there.

Another small charity which received the benefit of Frances' interest was the **Flower Mission**. Her main contribution for this was to raise funds. The first **Bewdley Mission** (see page 43), which was held in 1873, was planned and worked for by the Shaw family for a number of years. Again, Frances' support was mainly by supplying the music and training the choir. Frances was also involved in temperance work, an interest that she shared with Catherine Pennefather.

Cople

Cople was the village to which Henry was appointed as vicar. The name of Cople is derived from the Cock Pool, a place were chickens were kept; it was mentioned in the Domesday Book. The village is in Bedfordshire, 4 miles south-east of Bedford and is situated on the A603 between Bedford and Sandy, lying to the south of the A603. Buses 176, 177 and 178 operate on the A603 between Bedford and Sandy.

The church of All Saints, originally built in 1087, is in the centre of the village. The organ which Henry Havergal paid to have built during his time there as vicar is unusual in that it is an F organ, which is more suited to the human voice. There is easy wheelchair access and parking in adjacent lanes.

The church is described as one of the most beautiful in Bedfordshire. In its central position, it dominates the small village. The list of vicars dates back to 1237, including of course Henry East Havergal. It boasts a communion plate from around 1561, a 17th century sundial and six bells varying in date from the 14th century to early 20th century.

In the front garden of a private house next to the church can be seen the Bier House. This small building from the late 19th century was used to store the bier on which the coffins were wheeled into the church for funerals.

The few remaining places of interest are the Toll House dating from 1770 on the A603 and Cople House which was destroyed by fire in 1971 with only the original coach house remaining. These have been restored and renovated into three houses.

The nearest rail station is Bedford.

Upton Bishop

Upton Bishop is situated in the south-east corner of Herefordshire near Ross-on-Wye, between the M50, junction 3 to the south, the A449 to the north-west and the B4224 to the south-west. Appearing in the Domesday Book as Upton Episcopi, it has views of the Malverns, Cotswold Hills and the Forest of Dean.

Buses operate on the A449 between Ledbury and Ross-on-Wye. The nearest rail stations are Hereford and Gloucester. The church of St John the Baptist is situated in a narrow country lane with very limited parking.

St John the Baptist church was restored by Sir George Gilbert Scott in 1862.

The church is set in a churchyard which today has been carefully conserved to promote wildlife, including the marvellous wild 'Dymock daffodils' in season. The times of the church services are posted in the porch. The memorial to Frank Havergal is well positioned being on the left of the path as the church is approached through the lych-gate. The area is very rural with a scattered population. The building of the vestry in the 19th century resulted in the uncovering of medieval carved stones and an enigmatic fragment of what appears to be a Roman tombstone.

More information can be obtained from www. uptonbishop.org

ASTLEY CHURCH, THE RECTORY, AND CHURCHYARD.

The Early Home and Resting Place of F. R. H.   The Tomb is beneath the spreading fir tree.

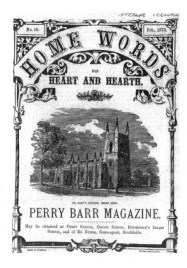

Top: *St Peter's Church and Rectory Astley, shortly after Frances' funeral in 1879*

Above right: *Rev W. H. Havergal, Frances' beloved father*

Above left: *Perry Barr, St John's church* Home Words *magazine frontspiece for February 1783*

⑦ 'Take my life'

Many a heart has been calmed, many a spirit uplifted and many a soul captured by the pen of this Worcestershire poetess and hymn writer

In 1864 Frances wrote to a friend: 'If I had my choice, I should like to be a Christian poetess.' It seems that Frances' desire was in line with God's will for her, as more and more of her work was being accepted. She became known as a hymn writer in her own right and not in the shadow of her father's name. When Frances received the idea for a hymn she did not delay, as proved by the speed with which 'Tell it out among the heathen' had been written. On one occasion she was visiting a boys' school with Rev Charles Snepp. Feeling tired she leaned against a wall while he went in to see the boys. When he returned about ten minutes later she handed him a piece of paper containing the hymn she had just written: 'Golden harps are sounding, angels voices ring, pearly gates are opened, opened for the King.'

Frances was only twenty-three when she spent the New Year with Maria, and listening to the church bells commented that the verse for the year would be 'As thy days, so shall thy strength be.' Frances, who was writing a card to a friend at the time, composed and added to the card the words of : 'Another year is dawning O Master let it be, in sleeping or in waking, another year for Thee.'

Others with similar themes were penned while she was away on holiday. 'I am trusting Thee Lord Jesus, trusting only Thee,

Above: *A Welsh harp drawn in Frances' autograph book, which is a copy of one on a brooch she used to wear. Frances used this as her personal emblem with the gold shamrocks and the whole design by an unknown artist. The first part of the Irish lettering reads: 'As the Father hath loved me, so have I loved you' John 15:9*

Facing page: *Paraclete Church, Newton, Mumbles. In Frances' day the village pump stood just beyond the boundary*

Above: *Areley House, Stourport, now a private residence, where Frances wrote her hymn 'Take my life…'*

trusting Thee for full salvation, full and free' was one of these hymns. This was written in 1874 at Ormond Dessus, Vaud in Switzerland, a country which was the origin of much of her work, and at a very productive period of her literary output. This hymn was included on the 12th day of the cycle for a month in *Loyal Responses*. The hymn was said to be one of her favourites, and proof of this was that a copy of it was found in her pocket Bible after her death.

An experience of the Holy Spirit

2 December 1873 proved to be very important in Frances' journey into holiness. Greatly influenced by the theology of the Keswick experience, Frances longed for a total commitment to God in a holy life. On that day she experienced a deeper outpouring of the Holy Spirit and it was a turning point of her spiritual life. In trying to describe it, she said to Maria: 'It is more distinct than my conversion; I can't date that. But what you see you can never unsee.' She had no doubt now about her response to God: 'I want to die for Him, but that could not be, so one wants to live for Him.' There was no longer the ebb and flow of her emotions. Soon after the event she was to pen the words:

'In full and glad surrender, I
  give myself to Thee,
Thine utterly and only, and
  evermore to be.
O Son of God, Who lov'st me I
  will be thine alone;
And all I have and am Lord,
  Shall henceforth be Thine
  own.'

This was written by Frances in the singular, not the plural. Anecdotally it is said to have been 'pluralised' for use in the United States.

Whenever she was fit enough, Frances continued with her writing, but in 1874 there was a major disaster. All her American publishing had been placed with one company. Therefore, when the company became bankrupt in that year, Frances' American hopes were dashed. At the time she had no other contacts in the States and lost money. It took Frances a long time to build up future contacts in America.

This added stress no doubt led to a downturn in her health. Never a very fit person, she was highly strung and 'Little Quicksilver' had been a good name for her. In November 1874 she became very ill again with a tendency to fever. It was likely that she had typhoid fever and her family and friends feared for her life. Even during her illness, Frances still strived to be pleasing to God: 'O, for a heart that never sins', was a cry wrung from her at this time. Not only did Frances rededicate her life on the anniversary of her confirmation which had been in Worcester Cathedral, she also reviewed her spiritual life at each New Year. This meant that a number of her hymns were written at this special time of the year.

1874 was also a year when Frances produced much of her writing. In February she was able to stay five days as a house guest at Areley House near Stourport with her friends Mr and Mrs Joseph Rogers, relatives of the Crane family, along with their seventeen year old son Joseph

Below: The Oval Room at Areley House where, in 1874, Frances wrote the hymn 'Take my life...'

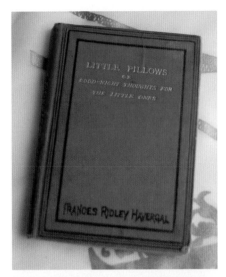

Left: Little Pillows *with the explanatory subtitle:* Good Night Thoughts for the Little Ones

each coming to know the Lord or re-consecrating themselves to him. She wrote in her diary that during the night of 4th February she was too excited to sleep and couplets kept forming in her mind. Sitting in the beautiful Oval Room the next day, the words of a hymn quickly formed in her mind. 'Take my life and let it be, consecrated Lord to Thee' is possibly the most well known of Frances' hymns today. In each verse she dedicated a different part of her body and her life to God, to be used for his glory. The first tune used was Patmos, composed by her father, but many other tunes have been used since.

Above: *Days 18 and 19 of the 3rd edition of* Little Pillows. *Frances often included one of her own poems*

Edmund, and their two daughters Mary Elizabeth, fifteen and Sarah Kate, thirteen. The house, situated on the outskirts of Stourport, was a fine 18th century building. Frances' time there was a period of great spiritual uplift for her. She prayed earnestly for all of the ten people staying in the house and was rewarded by

In her book *Kept for the Master's Use* Frances expounds more fully each verse of the hymn, and in this book she substituted the word *keep* for *take,* thus making it 'Keep my life, that it may be', and the next verse 'Keep my moments and my days', explaining that consecration is not so much a step as a course, not so much an act as a position to which a course of action inseparably belongs. She explained that we do not want to go on taking a first step again and again. So popular has this hymn become that it has been translated into French, German, Swedish, Russian and other European languages as well as several African and Asian dialects.

International fame

By this time, Frances was in constant demand for contributions to numerous evangelical periodicals, some in the USA and Canada. This is one of the reasons why Frances has such a large following in these countries today. She also worked tirelessly raising funds for her favourite charities, the Church Missionary Society (CMS) and the Irish Society. Also close to her heart was the Children's Special Services Mission (CSSM).

Having numerous nieces and nephews, Frances was well in touch with children and started to write for them. *Little Pillows* and its successor *Morning Bells* were both books which were popular and sold in large numbers. Many parents were eager to buy them for their children. In view of her emerging talent for writing for children, it was sad that she was not spared longer to continue to write for them.

Her books *My King, Royal Bounty* and *Royal Commandments* were all selling well. Her next book *Royal Invitation*, she described as 'for outsiders'. It was in the form of thirty-one texts and then a commentary in prose and occasionally some of her own verses. Most of the texts were from the Old Testament and then they were linked with the New Testament. This was a format which she used in other books. When *Royal Invitation* was published in 1878, 30,000 copies of *My King* were already in circulation. By this time two collections of Frances' poems had already appeared: *Ministry of Song* in 1871 and *Under the Surface* in 1874. All her work was receiving good reviews and she was amazed that everything seemed to be successful. Nevertheless *The Four Happy Days* and *Ben Brightboots* were two of her works which were not published until after her death. All through her life, alongside her books, poems and hymns, Frances dedicated much time to letter-writing; so much so that after her death Maria was able to gather many of the letters into a book. This book entitled simply *Letters* gave wonderful insights into Frances' life.

Too much correspondence

Frances also received many letters from those who benefitted from her work. When her mail was at its height, she was reduced to printing a circular letter to answer the most common questions:

'Dear…

Pardon me for regretfully resorting to this way of replying, as the continually increasing number of correspondents personally unknown to me, renders it simply impossible to send written answers to each. You will find a mark against the paragraph or sentence which contains a reply to your letter.'

Above: *The lych-gate leading to the Upton Bishop church*

Frances then lists nine of the commonly asked questions, but she was able to cope with all types of request. However, she did not intend to become a critic of other people's work, because she was too busy with her own writing. Those who requested a 'candid opinion' of their compositions were advised to send to a publisher, and never to self publish. Others tried to tell Frances what to write! To these she replied that her inspiration came from God. Some people were enquiring where they could obtain her work. They were referred to Nisbet & Co., her publishers in London. Some people complimented her on her work and were not expecting a reply; those she thanked profusely. She was humble in her achievements, giving all the glory to God. Frances realised that she was just a servant of God and she wished to dedicate her talent entirely to his service. She took no pride in her own achievements.

Fragile health

Frances' health, always fragile, had suffered a further blow when, on the way home from her Swiss holiday in 1874 she contracted typhoid. Returning home to Leamington Spa, Caroline nursed her and during this period there was no tension between the two ladies, as Caroline was extremely capable at nursing the sick. With this illness Frances suffered much pain and forced inactivity, yet by April 1875 she was beginning to recover; her doctor's advice was that she should not work for another six months. Frances had already ceased writing her many letters, and hymns were not composed and compositions were not worked on although in her diary she records that she did manage birthday acrostics for her nieces Cecilia and Edith Havergal.

Whitby instead of New York!

Frances had just one invitation to the States, to a YWCA Conference in New York in 1875. She was a faithful YWCA member for all her adult life. Unfortunately the further bout of illness in the summer of that year had intervened to prevent her going, and instead she was taken to Whitby in Yorkshire by Giles and Ellen Shaw, and her niece Frances Anna Shaw. They stayed at 14 Royal Crescent, in the style of similar crescents at both Bath and Buxton. Royal Crescent sits on Whitby's West Cliff and no 14 had an uninterrupted view of the sea.

At Whitby, Frances one day attended a midday prayer meeting. Here she heard a man

Below: The vestry at Upton Bishop church erected in memory of Frances. Frank also had a treble bell cast in her name, completing the peel of six

pray fervently 'Father, we know the reality of Jesus Christ.' Those words played over and over in her mind. Some two weeks later, on a very wild, stormy night, the lifeboat Harriott Forteath (the first of three boats to bear that name) was launched as there were ships in danger. Frances saw all of this and on 14 October 1875, she wrote the verses of 'Reality, Reality' including the reference to Christ as 'Pilot, lifeboat and haven.'

'Reality in greatest need,
Lord Jesus Christ, Thou art indeed!
Is the pilot real, who alone can guide
The drifting ship through the midnight tide?
Is the lifeboat real, as it nears the wreck,
And the saved ones leap from the parting deck?
Is the haven real, where the

Above: A cross stitch bookmark belonging to Frances

barque may flee
From the Autumn gales of the
  wild North Sea?
Reality, indeed art Thou,
My Pilot, Lifeboat,
  Haven now!'

In those days, when seaside visitors were fewer and thus more conspicuous, the local newspaper, the 'Whitby Gazette' regularly listed each week's visitors. The details of Frances and the Shaws appear in the editions of 25 September and 1 and 8 October 1875.

Then came a further blow for Frances. As she was being helped into the carriage to take her from Leamington Spa to Winterdyne for a short break to recuperate, a telegram arrived telling of the death of her brother Henry. She was so weak that it was decided not to tell her of his death until she had completed the journey. Frances then suffered a further relapse.

In 1875 Caswell & Co. printed a New Year card in which appeared 'Another Year is Dawning' which Frances had written the previous New Year, one of her almost annual New Year hymns. By April of the following year, Frances felt sufficiently strong to commence writing again, and set about editing the many pages of the appendix of *Songs of Grace and Glory* for the Hendersons Press. When she had completed this large task she sent it off to the printers and said joyfully to her sister: 'There, it is all done and now I am free to write a book.'

A disastrous fire

A week after her manuscript had been sent, at four o clock in the morning, the warehouse was destroyed by fire and with it her manuscript. The note from the printer said, 'Your musical edition, together with the paper you sent for printing it, has been totally destroyed.' Frances had no copy of the work and there was nothing to do but to spend much of the following year rewriting and revising *Songs of Grace and Glory*.

A further complication arose because the house at Leamington Spa was always closed up when Caroline and her friend, Miss Nott, travelled abroad. This left Frances homeless. Fortunately, the families at Winterdyne and Oakhampton were always pleased for Frances to stay with them. She also visited Henry's widow who

With most of her hymns, every line was backed up by a verse of Scripture, but this was especially true of the hymn 'I spent long years for thee' where she listed the biblical references she used:

'I spent long years for thee' ('Christ Jesus came into the world to save sinners; of whom I am the chief' 1 Timothy 1:15).

'In weariness and love' ('He is despised and rejected of men; a man of sorrows, and acquainted with grief' Isaiah 53:3).

'That an eternity' ('Thou lovedst me before the foundation of the world' John 17:24).

'Of joy thou mightest know' ('Your heart shall rejoice, and your joy no man taketh from you' John 16:22).

'I spent long years for thee' ('He was in the world, and the world was made by him, and the world knew him not. He came unto his own and his own received him not' John 1:10–11).

'Hast thou spent one for Me?' ('That he no longer should live the rest of his time in the flesh to the lusts of men, but to the will of God' 1 Peter 4:2).

The hymn continues with every line allotted its own verse of Scripture.

now lived with younger members of her family in Somerset. But of all the houses, Winterdyne was the best place for her to be, because Giles and Ellen realised that she needed peace and quiet to be able to work.

In June 1876 Frances went to stay with her brother Frank and his family at Upton Bishop vicarage. As was her custom, she involved herself in visiting schools and cottages in the village and joining in with the community.

At one well remembered service she accompanied herself on her brother's organ with works from *The Messiah*. She was also one of the first contributors towards the fund for the erection of a vestry (later named in her honour) which her brother was having built for the church.

Because of the disruptive nature of her home life, there were periods when Frances' productive output was small. Not many poems originated during

Left: *The church at Astley today is in urgent need of repair and a fund has been set up for this purpose*

this time at Leamington Spa, although many had been written in the previous ten year period. Nevertheless, after ten years' work, in 1879 she had published her fourth book of poems *The Ministry of Song*.

A sheltered life

Having spent all her years living with various members of her family, and brought up in a rectory, the life Frances led was inevitably sheltered. However, she visited the poor in their homes virtually throughout her life; although she never saw the inside of a theatre, but with the encouragement of her sisters, she cared passionately about the unfortunate. Frances gave generously to missionary work and when possible helped her family as they ministered to the

poor. But we must not assume that all this made her a dull person. In fact, Frances was just the opposite, described as having an 'infectious vivacity'. During her life she had many offers of marriage, but never felt it was God's will for her to accept any of them. Consequently she had time for extending her talents as she spent much time in prayer, composing and writing. Frances was disciplined in her reading, hardly ever having read a novel and only once since her school days venturing into Shakespeare. She wanted to spend her time on more worthwhile matters. Poetry was her only inclination, her favourites being Robert Browning, John Milton and George Herbert and on the inside back cover of her personal address book is the signature of the american poet Henry W. Longfellow, dated 1876. As we have seen, in her reading she had worked methodically through her father's library, and she read the Bible systematically and learned by heart large portions. It was no doubt this discipline of her time and reading which revealed itself in her writing. And it is for her hymn writing that Frances is best remembered today. Most of the music she composed is no longer in regular use today.

Much of her writing was printed in leaflet form by J & R Parlane, or made into ornamental cards by Caswell & Co. based in

Left: The re-gilded clock face at Astley church is still in evidence today

London. She would have her verses printed on the card with a space at the bottom for a signature, and at Christian meetings she would distribute these, hoping that the recipients would sign them as a confession of faith. It was only later that the verses were gathered together and published in small volumes: *Under the Surface, Loyal Responses, Life Mosaic* and *Life Chords*. A few years after her death, a fuller work was compiled posthumously under the title *Poetic Works* (1894).

One hymn which is still often sung today, 'Who is on the Lord's side?', was written on 13 October 1877. Frances thought of life as a battle and the Christian life as that of a soldier, and this battle hymn refers to the biblical story of the captains of the tribes of Israel giving allegiance to David after Saul's death at the hands of the Philistines (1 Chronicles 12). It was first published in *Loyal Responses* for the 5th day. At one time her own tune Hermas was used for it.

In the late 1870s Frances began to think about her future. When she was in Switzerland, she tried to plan what she should do. Although she was unwell some of the time, she still had opportunity to think without distractions. Maybe she should move away from Caroline and live with Ellen and Giles permanently. Maria had already moved to Bewdley, and Elizabeth Clay had gone to work overseas. Frances felt as if

Above: A plaque in the wall of Caswell Avenue stating that Frances Ridley Havergal lived here

Inset: The plaque in memory of Frances

Above: The popular sandy beach at Caswell Bay

everyone around her was moving. In the event she did nothing about it and 1877 passed fairly uneventfully, with her either visiting her brothers and sisters, or visiting London. Then in 1878 Caroline became very ill. This was a difficult time for Frances. She had been used to having family whom she could rely on. Now she was the one having to make decisions and organise the best care for Caroline.

Caroline and a new home

As Caroline became more unwell, Frances was the obvious one to nurse her. She remembered how good her stepmother had been to her during her own many illnesses. Maybe there was also a degree of guilt in her mind of any unkind thoughts she might

have harboured. Whatever the reason, Frances was a great help to Caroline in her final months. Caroline was subject to 'alarming attacks of severe prostration', and her degree of pain was such as to be distressing to those who cared for her. But throughout her last few weeks she was acutely aware of how much she was indebted to Frances and she managed to thank her on many occasions. The pain increased and it was a welcome release when she died on 26 May 1878. Caroline was buried beside her husband in the Astley churchyard. With Caroline gone, Maria and Frances had no alternative but to break up the family home.

After the strain of Caroline's illness, the sisters went away to the Mumbles to recover. Here they were joined by Frank. It was a time of emotional restoration and strengthening friendship for them all. When Frank returned to his home, it was decided that the ladies should take up lodgings with Mr and Mrs Tucker at Park Villa in Caswell Bay. This was to be their home for the rest of Frances' life. The first task was to sort out the old home in Leamington Spa prior to setting up residence in the Welsh village. They agreed that they would not take too many belongings with them. In the event Maria took plenty, while Frances took only a few of her most precious possessions. Frances wanted to take literally the words 'Take my silver and my gold, not a mite would I withhold.' Prayerfully, she decided to sell all her jewellery and use the money raised for the Church Missionary Society. All she kept was a portrait of her father, a pocket locket and the two rings which had been connected with her niece, Evelyn Crane. £50 was raised by the sale of this jewellery; a great deal of money considering her father's annual stipend at Shareshill had been only £29. Still needing to take holidays, in August the sisters spent some time with Henry's widow and family in Somerset, visited friends in Plymouth and Newport, and also had a period with the Shaws at Winterdyne.

Before long Maria and Frances were settling in at their new home. In her usual way Frances quickly became involved in the affairs of the neighbourhood. Rapidly the postman got to know that each day there would be a very heavy load of post for the Worcestershire poet. Many people were still seeking Frances' spiritual advice and corresponding about her work.

Below: The side view of Havergal House, Caswell; previously known as Park Villa

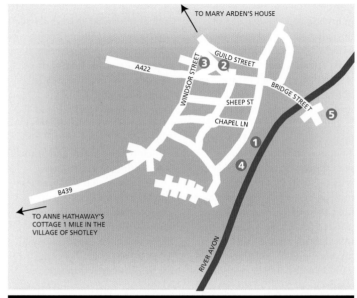

TO MARY ARDEN'S HOUSE

GUILD STREET

A422

WINDSOR STREET

BRIDGE STREET

SHEEP ST

CHAPEL LN

B439

TO ANNE HATHAWAY'S
COTTAGE 1 MILE IN THE
VILLAGE OF SHOTLEY

RIVER AVON

STRATFORD-UPON-AVON

1 ROYAL SHAKESPEARE
THEATRE

2 SHAKESPEARE'S
BIRTHPLACE

3 SHAKESPEARE CENTRE

4 SWAN THEATRE

5 TOURIST INFORMATION

TRAVEL INFORMATION

Stratford-upon-Avon

Stratford-upon-Avon is the birthplace of England's greatest poet and playwright and also an important market town in Warwickshire. A short walk round the town will pass most of the places of interest.

Commence at the Royal Shakespeare Theatre standing on the banks of the River Avon www.rsc.org.uk information ☎ 01789 403444. Go west along Chapel Lane. Many houses from the time of Shakespeare are still standing and in good condition, mainly due to the work of the Stratford Preservation Society.

Turn right into Chapel Street, the fine building of the Town Hall will be passed at the junction with Sheep Street. The roundabout ahead leads to a pedestrianised area containing Shakespeare's Birthplace ☎ 01789 204016 www.shakespeare.org.uk Limited mobility access and the Shakespeare Centre, both two minutes' walk from Wood Street. The library ☎ 01789 292209 & 01789 296 904. www.warwickshire. gov.uk/library in Henley Street has further local information (limited mobility access). The *Jester Statue* at the far end of the street is worth seeing.

Returning to the roundabout, Bridge Street leads to the river and over the bridge is the tourist information centre. For more information about the whole area www.shakespeare-country.co.uk or call ☎ 0870 1607930.

For information about Mary Arden's House, the mother of Shakespeare, call ☎ 01789 201806 or

*Top right: Mumbles'
lighthouse cut off
from the mainland by
the high tide. A scene
familiar to Frances*

*Right: A sketch drawn
in 1879 by Helga
von Cramm, of the
Mumbles' lighthouse
and heads. Frances
had first met Helga in
Switzerland*

*Bottom right: Wild
flowers along the
Gower cliffs*

www.shakespeare.org.uk.
Mary Arden's house is 2½
miles north of Stratford
off A3400.
☎ 01789 293455, *Anne
Hathaway's Cottage*,
☎ 01789 292100,
3 miles from Stratford off
the A46 and 2½ miles
from Mary Arden's House
in Wilmcote.

The River Severn

Having spent most of
her years near the River
Severn, Frances was
influenced by it in her life
and hymns. At 220 miles
long from source to sea,
it is the longest river in
England, although its
source is in the Cambrian
mountains in Wales,
and it joins the sea at
Bristol. It passes through
or close by the towns
of Shrewsbury, Telford,
Bridgnorth, Kidderminster,
Stourport-on-Severn,
Worcester and Gloucester,
before widening out at
Chepstow, Cardiff and
Weston-super-Mare. It is
calculated that the Severn
is crossed by about 100
bridges of various types.
The famous Severn Bore
is the second highest tide
anywhere in the world
with a range which can be
in excess of 50 ft.

The major road in the
region is the M5 which
goes in a north-south
direction, though many
A roads also connect
the various towns. The
railway routes link at such
stations as Birmingham,
Kidderminster, Worcester
in the north and
Gloucester in the south.

FRANCES RIDLEY HAVERGAL

8 'I did so want to glorify Him'

The talent that Frances had for putting her thoughts and compassion into words and verse lasted until the end of her life. Thousands were blessed by this talent during her life and millions after her death

By October 1878, Maria and Frances were settling into Wales. Frances felt so free at Mumbles: 'What emancipation!' she often exclaimed to Maria. Living in her own home at last, she was able to work hard at her writing, deal with her correspondence and often visit her publisher in London.

Frances was still an attractive and accomplished lady in her early forties, and was still receiving offers of marriage. She was never able to find another committed believer with whom she was willing to share the rest of her life. But she confided in one of her letters: 'It is not exactly or entirely feeling disappointment about – but more the sense of heart-loneliness and need of a one and special love… and the belief that my life is to be a lonely one in that respect.' She therefore prayed that she would find full contentment in her devotion to God.

Frances had a most comfortable study in their Caswell Bay home. A tidy worker, she kept all her papers in perfect order, and by her side was her harp-piano for her composing. On the other side she stored the many reference books and Bibles which helped her in her writing. The south window offered a view across the sea toward Ilfracombe in Devon, while from the west window the sunsets over Caswell Bay could be spectacular. Today her views would not be so unrestricted; they would be blocked by tall trees and newer buildings. Frances kept to her lifelong rule of rising early

Above: *The hallway of Havergal House, now privately owned, where except for the central heating, little has changed since the days of Frances and Maria*

Facing page: *A framed photograph of Frances Ridley Havergal hanging in the updated hall of the Paraclete Church at Newton, South Wales*

Caswell Bay

The part of Mumbles where Maria and Frances lived was known as Newton, and the nearest beach was a short walk down the steep hill to Caswell Bay. The name Caswell may have come from Cresswell or cress stream from the old English words 'cerse' (cress) and 'wella' (well). The Bay first became popular in Victorian times as a place for underprivileged workhouse children to visit. The famous also liked to visit. At one stage it became a summer residence for Henry Fox Talbot, who was noted as the inventor of the negative/positive photographic process. Today sandy Caswell Bay is one of the most popular of the Gower beaches for surfing, angling and family outings. The bay also has parking facilities and a nature reserve named Bishop's Wood.

Above: Mumbles lighthouse at low tide on a misty day

Failing health

Ever since suffering from typhoid in 1874, Frances had been subject to feverish attacks and these attacks were becoming more and more frequent. On Christmas morning 1878, Frances had severe pain and recorded: 'O Lord, prepare me for all Thou art preparing for me.' She recalled the words that her dying mother had requested her to pray, and now felt that God had answered that prayer. Mrs Charles Bullock had sent her a Christmas present of a little diary *Journal of Mercies 1879* and during the first three months of the year Frances kept brief entries. Her health did not allow her to write much more. But what she did write gave an insight into her prayer life: 'being enabled to cast care on God', 'having money to give away', 'Maria's writing letters for me.' That last entry reflected a blessing. There

and going to bed early, but in her contentment she often worked too hard with her writing as well as her temperance work, which was becoming more and more important in her life. This habit of driving herself was often to the detriment of her work and definitely to the detriment of her health. In her frequent times of working while resting in her bed, she was accompanied by her faithful kittens, Trot and Dot.

was still a large daily delivery of mail and Frances was not always strong enough to cope. Maria, on the other hand, felt it a privilege to be able to help her weak sister in this way.

Although more often confined to the house, Frances was not lonely at this time. She had many visitors. One of the most frequent was Baroness Helga von Cramm, whom Frances had met three years earlier in Switzerland.

Actually the visit was often of a business nature, because the Baroness was illustrating some of Frances' books and there was much to discuss. Two other visitors were Mr and Mrs Ira D Sankey. Sankey was an American gospel singer and composer who, along with Dwight L Moody, had conducted Christian campaigns in their home country of America, as well as in England and Scotland. Their following

Above: The rear garden of Havergal House

Right: Visitors on the road to Caswell Bay will pass by the reminder of Frances

Paraclete Congregational Church

The Paraclete Church in Newton, Caswell Bay, was where Frances and Maria worshipped for the very short period before Frances' death. It was one of six chapels established in Gower in the early part of the 1800s by Lady Diana Barham who recognised the needs of the people in the community and sought to improve their spiritual and material lives. Today the vision of the church remains the same, which reads: 'We recognise society's need. We can tell them and show them where that need can be met.' A thriving church today, it has been extended recently including the building of a new kitchen, toilet, shower and disabled toilets. This extension, renamed 'The Havergal Centre' in memory of Frances, has her picture hanging prominently over the piano as a reminder of the pride the church feels in her short stay with them at the end of her life.

Right: The reading desk in the Paraclete Church donated in memory of Frances

Below: The plaque on the reading desk in Paraclete Church

TO THE GLORY OF GOD AND IN MEMORY OF FRANCES RIDLEY HAVERGAL WHO WORSHIPPED IN THIS CHURCH. DEDICATED 1939.

in every country had been great. Ira greatly admired Frances' hymn writing, though Frances was not so keen on his *Songs and Solos*. Nevertheless, she greatly appreciated his friendship. When Frances had been very ill on a previous occasion, Mr Sankey had prayed for her while he was in Dublin and had urged others to pray as well. On this his final visit to the Welsh village, his words to Frances were, 'We'll meet again.' It was not to be in this life.

On 28 January 1879, Frances had been strong enough to visit her publishers in London, and while there she wrote to Maria about 'the pure and holy love which has been laid at my feet.' She had received yet another offer of marriage. This was to be the last of many. She was pleased to return to the sanctuary of South Wales.

Frances continued to visit the village school as strength permitted, and urged others to pray with her for an outpouring of the Holy Spirit on the people there. Wherever Frances lived she became fully integrated into the community, engaging with the people and telling of the gospel whenever there was opportunity. In March, she was able to spend time writing, and rewrote and completed her last book *Kept*, and a series of papers for invalids. She was still writing and correcting musical scores and her volume of work did not decrease, although her strength did. Her interest in temperance work was a fairly new outlet for her passion, but it increasingly took up more of her time and strength.

At Easter 1879 Elizabeth Clay, home from the Punjab, visited and shared her experiences of the time in India. The two ladies had an enjoyable Easter together as they recalled their previous adventures during their holidays in Europe. But those times seemed a long time away now. Elizabeth had served abroad as a missionary and Frances was rapidly becoming an invalid. For the Easter service, Frances walked to church for almost the last time, but it took more strength than she possessed.

Final days

Baroness Helga von Cramm came to visit again at the beginning of May and remarked that Frances seemed quite well, though she noticed that she often felt weak. On 21 May, Frances had promised to meet some of the boys and men by the village green. Whatever her state of health she could never miss an opportunity for witness. She would have been wiser to have stayed at home as the day was chilly and wet, and in the event she was so tired that she had to ride a donkey back home. But still she continued to witness to various people in the village, although by now she had a feverish cold.

On 24 May the Baroness left, although she was still not unduly worried about Frances' state of health. However, during the

Above: *The interior of the Paraclete Church today where Frances worshipped for such a short period*

next few days Frances became extremely ill and the doctor was called. Frances asked him, 'Do you think I have a chance of going?' and he replied that she was not seriously ill. By 29 May it was obvious that the illness was more serious than the feverish attacks to which she was so prone. The doctor diagnosed that Frances was ill with peritonitis and typhoid. Sarah Carveley, who had nursed Caroline, was sent for. Maria continued to read letters to her, until Frances felt too ill to hear any more. She had constant sickness and agonizing pain and, realising that her life could not last much longer, she asked for her brother Frank to visit and they talked about old times. She needed to remember when life had been more pleasant.

The text in Frances' room read 'The blood of Jesus Christ His Son cleanseth us from all sin.' She gained comfort just by reading it, and when the doctor was leaving on his next visit, she asked again, 'Will I be going today?' On being told 'Probably', she replied 'Beautiful, too good to be true' and 'splendid to be so near the gate of heaven.' She had had enough of living and suffering.

When Frances was a young child, her godmother Elizabeth Cawood, had commented, 'I believe that child will die singing.' The prediction was true. With her family grouped round her, she tried to sing the words 'Jesus, I will trust Thee, trust Thee with my soul' to her own tune *Hermas*. Her weak voice faltered and Ellen took over the singing. Maria was able to lean forward and catch

Top: *The pier at Mumbles which was not built until the 1900s*

Above: *The Mumbles lighthouse known to Frances*

her last words: 'I did so want to glorify Him every step of the way.' The release came on 3 June 1879 as Frances Ridley Havergal passed into glory. She had packed a great deal into her forty-two years.

Top: Newton in the days of Frances, showing the pump standing outside the Paraclete Church

Above: Newton village in the days of Frances

The funeral

Frances' funeral was on Monday 9 June 1879 at 6 pm; it was common in Victorian times for funerals to be in the evening. On that day there was a storm in the morning, though the sun burst through the clouds in the afternoon as the birds began to sing. Frances had wanted a cheerful funeral and it was so. The coffin was brought by train from Swansea to Stourport

Above: A copy of the burial record for Frances on the wall of Astley church

Left: The steps leading to St Peter's, Astley where Frances' body was carried to her final resting place

on Severn railway station. There a horse-drawn hearse was waiting and this conveyed the coffin through the streets of the town and then along country lanes to St Peter's Church Astley; here, at the Rectory she had been born just 42 years and 6 months earlier. Years later a passer by in Foundry Street recalled the scene: 'The sight riveted me. It was not a funeral cortege with the black nodding plumes typical of those far-off days, but instead, a car of triumph, gaily dressed with wreaths of laurels, and on the coffin itself a golden star of Banksia roses and a poet's wreath of laurel and bay.' The Kidderminster Shuttle explained why: 'Her hope was a bright and joyous one, and she wished things to be in accordance with her hope.'

The mourners wore white waistcoats and white kid gloves. Her body was transported to the Astley churchyard, where she was buried in the marble tomb beside her father and stepmother.

Under the tree which Canon Havergal had planted so many years before, she was finally laid to rest. The tombstone already bore the inscription for her father along half of the top side: 'The Rev William Henry Havergal MA, vicar of Shareshill and Canon of Worcester, died at Leamington 19 April 1870 aged 77. Curate and rector 13 years of this parish 1822 to 1842, a faithful minister in the Lord.'

Along one of the sides were the words commemorating his first wife: 'Jane, 5th daughter of Wm Head died 5 July 1848 aged(too worn to be read) and was buried in St Nicholas Church, Worcester.' The other side of the tomb bears the words: 'His second wife Caroline Anne daughter of John Cooke died at Leamington 26 May 1878 aged 65.' The second half of the top of the tomb bears the inscription for Frances: 'Frances Ridley Havergal youngest daughter of the Revd William Havergal and Jane his wife. Born at Astley rectory 14 Dec 1836 died at Caswell Bay Swansea 3 June 1879 aged 42. By her writings in prose and verse she being dead yet speaketh.' As she had requested, the following words were also added: 'The blood of Christ, His Son, cleanseth us from all sin' 1 John 1:7. This was the text which had been hanging in her room as she died.

Epitaphs

Many epitaphs were uttered on learning of her death. One said, 'The loss to the church of Christ is not easily estimated.' A college set up in Toronto for 600 students was named the Havergal College in memory of Frances. In Ontario, a post office was rebuilt using her name. After Frances died, friends in Leamington set up the Havergal Memorial Building Fund which was to be devoted to the work of the Irish Society. In the event this did not prove very successful, although a Havergal Memorial Hall was set up in Limerick in a building which had been a Masonic Hall. This was then used for 'mission services, sermons or addresses in Irish, ragged and mission schools (Sundays and weekdays), and other purposes of the Irish Society.' The hall was finally closed in 1950 and the funds were transferred to 'educational purposes'. The portrait of Frances, which had been in the hall, was moved to the Trinity Home for the Blind in Limerick.

In June that year Frances had planned to go to Ireland and had been greatly looking forward to

Above: *Flowers laid on the tomb of Frances to commemorate Havergal Day. Yellow was believed to be her favourite colour*

the visit. Instead the poet was being laid to rest, though not to be forgotten. Ironically, one of the last books she wrote was especially for invalids, *Starlight Through the Shadows*. *Marching Orders* concludes with the hymn 'Who is on the Lord's side.'

Left:The corner of Astley churchyard where the Havergals are buried

Certain books and articles of Frances' were not published until after her death. The 1880 YWCA almanac carried an article by her, and for all who read it, it was a sad reminder of their great loss. After her death the money that was given in her memory was used to set up the Havergal Memorial Building Fund, to be used for missionary work; an arrangement she would have approved, church missionary work being close to her heart. By February 1880, 12,000 contributors had given a total of £1,900.

Above: A procession in the Astley churchyard to mark Havergal Day in 2007. She is remembered each year on the nearest Sunday to her death

The legacy of Frances

Maria wrote: 'My sister's books are not about religion, but about the Lord Jesus as a personal living Saviour.' She wanted her talented sister to be remembered, and therefore in 1881 published *Memorials of Frances Ridley Havergal*, using her own recollections and drawing on letters which Frances had written and those which had been written to her. So popular was this book that the first 18,000 copies were immediately repeated. Maria lived another eight years after her sister, dying in 1887. Twenty years later 250,000 copies of the book had been distributed.

However, the greatest memorial to Frances, her work and her life, is her hymns, many of which are still sung today. Many hearts have been uplifted by their direct style and simple words. In her lifetime, it was her writings that were most revered; today it is the words of her hymns. The total number of hymns which Frances wrote was about seventy. Whenever Frances wrote a hymn, she would usually compose a matching tune. The most well known in use today is *Hermas*. Occassionally, she used tunes her father had composed. Many items written by Frances have survived the changes in congregational singing. When today, congregations sing, 'Take my life and let it be' or 'Who is on the Lord's side?', sadly too few know anything of the author.

Frances had finally achieved her desired wish which she expressed in her hymn 'Take myself and I will be, ever only all for Thee.'

Annual memorial

One place where Frances is remembered and revered is St Peter's Church at Astley where she was born and where she is laid to rest. Every year on the first Sunday in June (the one nearest the date of her death) a special Havergal Day is held. In 2004 it was the 125th anniversary of her death, which made the day even more special. Many admirers from America as well as from England made the pilgrimage to remember her.

In 2007 the service consisted, as always, of a procession to lay a floral tribute on her tomb. All the hymns in the service were hers. The procession passed many of the trees which her father had planted and which she would have remembered in her lifetime. 'Take my life and let it be' was the first hymn to be sung. To the right stood the Rectory where Frances had spent her first few happy years. Later during the service, the strains of the lesser known hymn 'O Saviour, precious Saviour' filled the church. This was followed by her hymn: 'Jesus, Master, whose I am' which revealed the lovely lines of dedication: 'Let my heart be all Thine own, let me live to Thee alone', and words which now she was proving: 'Whom have I in heaven but Thee? Nothing else my joy can be.' Finally, in strident tones the question was asked in song: 'Who is on the Lord's side?'

Left: Stourport on Severn Railway Station very much as it was around the time of Frances' funeral in 1879. Her coffin was brought here by train on the day of her funeral

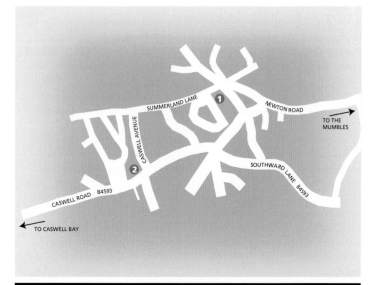

NEWTON AND CASWELL BAY

1 PARACLETE CHURCH

2 HAVERGAL HOUSE

TRAVEL INFORMATION

Swansea and Mumbles

This is the area where Frances spent the last few months of her life. It has been popular since Victorian times, as evidenced by the Mumbles Pier. Mumbles is at the southern end of Swansea Bay and the gateway to the Gower Peninsula. The Norman keep of Oystermouth Castle dominates the hilltop behind the town. A selection of interesting shops, boutiques, galleries and potteries along the coastal road is an attraction to visitors.

Mumbles Tourist Information Centre, the Methodist Church, Mumbles Road, Mumbles, Swansea, SA3 4BU
☎ 01792 361302.
www.mumbles.co.uk
Open Mon-Sat 1–4 all year round.

The area can be reached by road via the M4 and A483. Swansea Station is served by trains from London Paddington, Bristol, Manchester and Cardiff. The nearest airport is Cardiff International Airport ☎ 01446 711111. www.cardiffairport.com

There is a ferry sailing between Cork and Swansea (currently suspended).
☎ 01792 474354.
Irish Ferries (Pembroke o Rosslare)
☎ 08705 171717.
www.irishferries.com
Stenaline (Fishguard to Rosslare)
☎ 08705 707070.
www.stenaline.co.uk

Frequent buses connect the area to all parts of the Gower. Traveline Cymru ☎ 0871 2002233. www.traveline-cymru.org.uk

Swansea Tourist Information Centre, Plymouth Street, Swansea SA1 3QG
☎ 01792 468321.
www.visitswanseabay.com

The Gower Heritage Centre
☎ 01792 371206.

www.
gowerheritagecentre.
co.uk

The Dylan Thomas
Centre, Somerset Place,
Swansea SA1 1RR
☎ 01792 463980.
www.dylanthomas.com

Caswell Bay

Caswell Bay is reached
from The Mumbles by
travelling west along the
B4593. There is parking
very close to the beach,
with refreshments from
a kiosk right next to the
sands. The nature reserve
is close by the parking
area. It is possible that
Maria and Frances would
have collected lava bread
seaweed from the bay
which could be boiled and
mixed with flour, oats and
black pepper. It would
then have been fried
with Welsh bacon fat and
cockles. In various places
round the Gower this
seaweed is still collected.
Lava bread seaweed
is very rich in iodine
and helpful in thyroid
disorders.

Paraclete Church

The word *paraclete*
appears five times in
the Bible and means
advocate. It is a reference
to the Holy Spirit. Built in
1818, the church was the
fourth of six chapels in the
Gower Peninsula, erected
by Diana, Lady Barham.
For the nine months
Frances was living in the
area she helped in the
Sunday school and played
the organ.

The church is situated
in Newton Road, Mumbles
☎ 01792 367811
For further information
about the church see
www.themumblesbook.
co.uk.

Above: *The tomb of
Giles and Ellen Shaw*

Left: *The separate
headstone of Maria
in the graveyard at
Astley. She is buried
in the Havergal
family grave*

Significant dates in the life of Frances Ridley Havergal

1836	**14 December** Frances Ridley Havergal born.
1842	Moved with her family from Astley to Hallow.
1842	**5 October** Miriam, her eldest sister was married.
1845	Moved with her family to St Nicholas, Worcester.
1846	Started Sunday School work.
1848	Jane, her mother died. Brother Henry married.
1850	**15 August** Started at Belmont School.
1850	Her father remarried to Caroline Cooke.
1851	Went to Powick School.
1852	First visit to Germany with her parents.
1853	The family moved to Lansdowne Crescent, Rainbow Hill.
1854	**17 July** Confirmed in Worcester Cathedral.
1856	**5 February** Sister Ellen married to Giles Shaw and moved to Ireland.
1856	First visit of Frances to Ireland.
1859	Family moved to Shareshill.
1860	Because of pressure of work, Frances finished Sunday School teaching.
1860	Ellen and Giles finally left Ireland. Brother Frank married.
1861	Received her first cheque for her poems.
1867	Father retired to Pyrmont Villa, Leamington Spa.
1868	Niece Evelyn Crane died.
1870	**19 April** William Henry Havergal, her father, died.
1871	*The Ministry of Song*, first volume of poems, published.
1871	Visited the Alps with Elizabeth Clay.
1872	At Winterdyne Frances wrote 'Lord, speak to me, that I may speak'.
1873	Visited Switzerland with the Snepp family.
1873	Received a further outpouring of the Holy Spirit.
1874	Work and money lost through the crash of her American publisher.
1874	A further visit to Switzerland.
1874	Work lost through fire at the publishers, Hendersons Press
1874	Wrote *Under the Surface*.
1874	Wrote 'Take my life and let it be' at Areley House.
1875	Brother Henry died.
1876	Last visit to Switzerland.
1877	Niece Miriam died.
1877	Wrote 'Who is on the Lord's side?'
1878	**26 May** Caroline, her stepmother, died.
1878	Moved to the Mumbles.
1879	**3 June** Frances died at home with her family.

Above: *The organ in St Peter's church restored in memory of William Havergal*

Select List of Hymns, Poems etc.

Thy life was given for me	January 1858
Jesus, Master, whose I am	December 1865
I bring my sins to Thee	June 1870
O Saviour, precious Saviour, whom yet unseen we love	November 1870
Sit down beneath His shadow	27 November 1870
Golden Harps are sounding	December 1871
O fill me with Thy fulness, Lord	1872
Lord speak to me, that I may speak	April 1872
Tell it out among the heathen that the Lord is King	April 1872
O Thee, O comforter divine	August 1872
I could not do without Thee	7 May 1873
Thou art coming, O my Saviour	16 November 1873
Will ye not come to Him for life	21 December 1873
Another year is dawning	April 1874
I am trusting Thee Lord Jesus	September 1874
Like a river glorious	November 1874
Take my life and let it be	4 February 1874
Master, how shall I bless Thy name	1876
Who is on the Lord's side?	October 1877
I spent long years for thee	
Now my evening praise I give	
O Jesus Christ my Master, I come to Thee today	
Oh, Thine for ever, what a blessed thing	17 July 1854 on the day of her confirmation
Who shall tell our untold need?	Poem January 1866
In God's great field of labour	Poem 27 February 1867
Upon the Word I rest each pilgrim day	Poem written a few weeks before her death
Sacred Songs for Little Singers	12 poems for children
Dear Blind Sister over the Sea	10 May 1872 A poem for Fanny Crosby

Publications by Frances Ridley Havergal

The Ministry of Song	1871
Bruey	1871
The Four Happy Days	1874
Under the Surface	1874
Little Pillows	1875
Morning Bells	1875
My King	1877
Royal Bounty	1877
Royal Commandments	1877
Loyal Responses	1878
Royal Invitation	1878
Echoes from the Word	1879
Kept for the Master's Use	1879
Morning Stars	1879
Under His Shadow	1879
Life Mosaic	1879

Published after her death

Swiss Letter	1881 (ed Jane Miriam Crane)
Ben Brightboots & other True Stories	1882
Life Echoes	1883
Poetical Works	1884

Picture acknowledgements

The following pictures are reproduced with grateful acknowledgment.

Reproduced by permission of the City and County of Swansea

Page 102	Caswell Bay
Page 112	The Mumbles lighthouse and pier

Reproduced by permission of Worcester Cathedral

Page 40	Clasp of FRH Bible
Page 40	FRH Bible
Page 41	Annotations from her Bible
Page 57	William Havergal's bust in Psalmody
Page 68	Havergal's Psalmody

Dr Keith White

Page 69	North Wales

J&M Bowdler

Page 53	Binswood Terrace, Leamington Spa
Page 55	St Paul's, Leamington Spa

David Marlow

Page 36	Winterdyne House
Page 43	Winterdyne House
Page 57	The lounge at Winterdyne House
Page 123	Whitby

Brian Edwards

Pages 62–65	Switzerland
Page 71	Jungfrau
Page 75	The Worcester and Birmingham Canal

Joy Piper

Page 52	Royal Commandments

Acknowledgements

In addition to many who have contributed to this book, the author would like especially to acknowledge the valuable advice of David Marlow whose interest and research into the life of Frances Ridley Havergal has been of great assistance.

A selection of books on the life of Frances Ridley Havergal

Memorials of F.R.Havergal,
M. V.G.Havergal, James Nisbet & Co 1880
Frances Ridley Havergal, T.H.Darlow,
Nisbet & Co Ltd London 1927
Frances Ridley Havergal, Esther E Enock,
Pickering & English Ltd 1937
The Sisters Charles Bullock B.D.
'Home Word' publishing Office
Christian Hymn Writers, Elsie Houghton,
Evangelical Press of Wales 1982
Frances Ridley Havergal, Janet Grierson,
Ebenezer Baylis & Son Ltd.
Published by the Havergal Society
to mark the centenary of the hymn
writer's death
Ever, only, all for Thee,
Pamela Bugden, Granted Ministries
Press 2010

The Havergal Trust is building an interesting website that reproduces some of her lesser known work and is well worth visiting: www.havergaltrust.com

The author

Carol Purves is the author of *Chinese Whispers,* the life story of Gladys Aylward, a missionary to China in the 1930s and *From Prussia with Love,* the account of George Müller, founder of the children's homes in Bristol, both published by Day One Publications.

A member of the Society of Authors and the Association of Christian Writers, Carol has written a number of meditations and articles on various subjects. She now lives in the beautiful city of Carlisle, where as a walker and photographer, she appreciates the closeness of the Lake District, the North Pennines and the Scottish Borders. Carol is a member of Hebron Evangelical Church in the city, working with the young people and a musician in one of their worship groups.

Below: *Royal Crescent, Whitby.*
See page 97

DAY ONE TRAVEL GUIDES

The Day One Travel Guide series introduces our Christian heritage through people and places that have been influential in the history of western civilization and far beyond. They introduce the lives of great Christian leaders, past and present, and tour lands and cities with a strong biblical connection. Attractively produced with around 150 informative drawings and photographs. A tour guide to introduce the places associated with the subject. Equally valuable for the armchair traveler they bring people and places alive.

- **PLACES OF INTEREST**

- **PACKED WITH COLOUR PHOTOS**

- **CLEAR ILLUSTRATED MAPS**

- **GREAT GIFT IDEA**

- **128 PAGES**

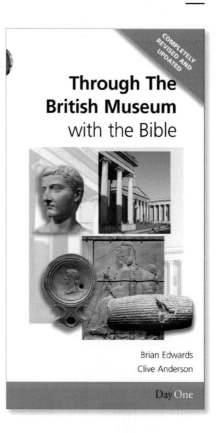

OTHER TITLES IN THIS SERIES

Travel with...

JOHN BUNYAN
C H SPURGEON
WILLIAM BOOTH
JOHN KNOX
MARTYN LLOYD-JONES
WILLIAM GRIMSHAW
WILLIAM CAREY
WILLIAM WILBERFORCE
C S LEWIS
ROBERT MURRAY McCHEYNE
MARTYRS OF MARY TUDOR
JOHN CALVIN
WILLIAM TYNDALE
JOHN BLANCHARD
BILLY GRAHAM

Travel through...

THE BRITISH MUSEUM
OXFORD
CAMBRIDGE
ISRAEL
EGYPT

MORE TITLES ARE IN PREPARATION

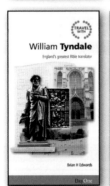

A series of children's activity books twinned with the Travel Guides

ROMANS, GLADIATORS AND GAMES
In the British Museum, explore the Roman world of the first Christians.

KINGS, PHARAOHS AND BANDITS
In the British Museum, explore the world of Abraham to Esther.

WILLIAM TYNDALE
He was threatened, hunted, betrayed and killed so that we could have the Bible in English

Permission is given to copy the activity pages and associated text for use as class or group material

EGYPT
Ancient Egypt and the Bible

JOHN BUNYAN
How a hooligan and soldier became a preacher, prisoner and famous writer

WILLIAM CAREY
The story of a country boy and shoe mender whose big dreams took him to India

WILLIAM BOOTH
The troublesome teenager who changed the lives of people no one else would touch

WILLIAM WILBERFORCE
The millionaire child who worked so hard to win the freedom of African slaves.

C S LEWIS
The story of one of the world's most famous authors who sold over a hundred million books

FRANCES' ENGLAND, WALES AND IRELAND

1 LONDON
2 WORCESTER
3 LEAMINGTON SPA
4 STRATFORD ON AVON
5 CHELTENHAM
6 SHARESHILL, CANNOCK

7 SWANSEA
  MUMBLES
  CASWELL
8 DUBLIN
9 CELBRIDGE LODGE
10 NORTH WALES

11 WHITBY
12 NORTH WORCESTERSHIRE
  - KIDDERMINSTER
  - ASTLEY
  - BEWDLEY

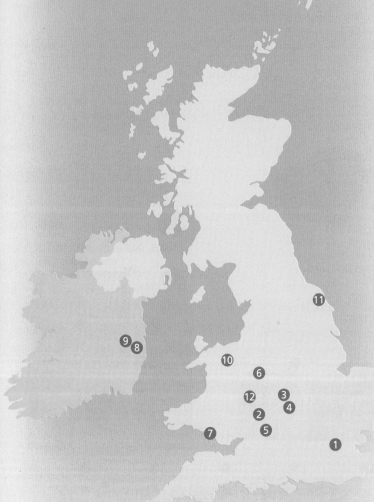